Charles J. Butler

A Bachelor's rambles through the British Isles

Charles J. Butler

A Bachelor's rambles through the British Isles

ISBN/EAN: 9783337216818

Printed in Europe, USA, Canada, Australia, Japan

Cover: Foto ©Andreas Hilbeck / pixelio.de

More available books at **www.hansebooks.com**

A Bachelor's Rambles

THROUGH

The British Isles.

By Chas. J. Butler.

CAMDEN, N. J.:
LOUIS B. COX, PRINTER, 764 FEDERAL ST.
1895.

To my Friends
on both sides of the broad Atlantic,
This Book
is affectionately dedicated by the author,
Chas. F. Butler.

Camden, New Jersey, 1895.

PREFACE.

WHEN I was a small boy we lived near a family who came from County Wicklow, Ireland. I was always intensely interested in hearing them describe the beauties of that country. A desire took hold of me to see the land beyond the broad Atlantic. This desire grew stronger as I heard and read descriptions of the British Isles in later years, but I always considered Old Ocean rather treacherous, and never felt like trusting myself to her care. Not until within a few months prior to taking the trip did I begin to think more favorably of her. The Sunday previous to sailing was very stormy, and calculated to make one rather pensive who was about to launch out on the uncertainties of the great deep. I spent a part of the day with some friends, one of whom, seating himself at the organ, began playing and singing for my especial benefit. His selections were of such a character as to make me feel I was spending my last Sabbath on earth; that somewhere between dear old America and the shores of England, Old Ocean would cover me over and keep me hidden away until Gabriel blew his trumpet. However, I was undaunted by the dark picture presented, and took the never-to-be-regretted trip, my enjoyment of which, together with some historic facts, I have endeavored, in my homespun way, to bring before my readers. C. J. B.

November 3, 1895.

The "Southwark."

By Chas. J. Butler.

The "Southwark," noble ship, came forth
  Old Ocean's waves to breast,
Just as the golden light of day
  Was sinking in the west.

Soon Night her sable mantle spread
  Out o'er our trackless way;
The stars peeped out, and o'er us watched
  'Till breaking of the day.

Old Ocean kindly smiled on us;
  She scarcely heaved a sigh;
She seemed just like a happy lass,
  When naught of care is nigh.

But, ah, the winds from far away,
  Some secret trouble brought;
She sighed, and moaned and cried aloud,
  As for relief she sought.

But still our noble ship pressed on,
  Her mission to perform;
To bear those trusted to her care,
  Safe through the raging storm.

Safe in the harbor now, at last,
  Our ship doth calmly rest,
Just as a little wearied child
  Sleeps on its mother's breast.

Thou, Ruler of the land and sea,
  Thanks unto Thee, who gave
To man the power to guide our ship
  Safe through each crested wave.

Written at Sea, June, 1895.

A Bachelor's Rambles Through the British Isles.

Seaward Bound.

WEDNESDAY, May 23, 1894, I embarked on the new and well-equipped steamer "Southwark," sailing from Philadelphia to Liverpool, England. When I purchased my ticket I was assigned to room No. 19, and had my luggage snugly packed away there for the voyage. Some of my friends who came to bid me adieu wished to see my quarters, so I led the way to the stateroom, and was about entering when the old Scotch steward called to me and said : "My lad, there is a woman and some children in that room." I said to him, "how is that?" I knew I had made no contract like that ; it was rather a heavy responsibility for a bachelor to assume the care of a lady and three children on a voyage of three thousand miles. I said : "My ticket calls for 19." "And so does the lady's," he replied. Sure enough, she was there with the trio, holding the fort. We hurried off on the wharf to see the agent. He informed me they were compelled to make a change, and neglected to notify me. I was given one of the officers' rooms on the outside of the ship, which was preferable to the one I had been assigned.

When I grasped the hands of my friends and bade them farewell, a strong desire took hold of me to gather up my bundles and go ashore with them, but I knew if I did, I should have to go into exile out in the Jersey pines, or be subject to the sport of those to whom I had talked of the trip so enthusiastically. A feeling of sadness crept over me as I saw the last line cast off, and we slowly drifted away from the grand old city with which I have been so familiar the most of my life. We steamed down the river, expecting to reach the Capes about 5 P. M., but when opposite Marcus Hook, Pa., we dropped anchor. The question was passed from one to another: "What is the matter?" Finally some one reported: "They are making some repairs to the engine." Just a few days before sailing I was introduced by my friend, Dr. S———r, to Mr. A——— M——— and wife, of Philadelphia, and to Mrs. D——— and family, of Cleveland, O. Aside from them, I knew no one on shipboard. Both families were returning to Nottingham, England, to make that their home again. We saw the sun drop down behind the western hills, and our ship still in the same position, with little prospect of leaving soon. One of the Miss D———'s played several piano solos for us, and the evening was passed very pleasantly. I retired at 10:30; could still see the lights along the shores of Pennsylvania and New Jersey. The pilot who was to take us as far as the Capes roomed with me. He said he thought we would leave about 1 A. M., on the high water. In conversation with him, I learned that he was a Mr. B———, of Cape May City, and was acquainted with a number of my friends. I told him I was feeling rather blue. He said he thought I would soon change color.

THURSDAY, May 24.—I was awakened about 3 A. M. by some one calling for the pilot. When he returned he said we would not be able to leave until the dense fog lifted. When I arose I found the heavy mist hiding the land from our view. I formed the acquaintance of Dr. R——, a son of one of the prominent ministers of the Philadelphia Conference. He was alone, and in the same frame of mind as myself— inclined to look back toward home and talk of the friends there. He was going to England and Germany to complete his education. He proved to be a very genial companion. When the gong sounded the invitation for dinner I had a good opportunity of seeing the ship's company. There were about 180 cabin passengers. Most of them I found to be very excellent people. Quite a number were from the West. The tables were laden with a good supply of food, and the steward, with his efficient corps of assistants, gave us the best of attention. The officers were kind, obliging men. I began to feel we were in a good, seaworthy ship, and one that was well manned; and it proved to be so. They lifted the huge piece of iron that had held us fast for nearly twenty-four hours, and we started seaward. We soon passed all the familiar towns on the Delaware and were in the broad bay, with the prospect of a kind reception from Old Ocean. But we had not proceeded far before I discovered a very ominous looking cloud in the southwest. The lightning soon began to flash and the thunder roll, and I concluded the elements were about to give us a grand sendoff. I had begun a correspondence with some who were especially interested in the tall lad of more than thirty summers; the pilot kindly consented to post my letters. When we reached the Breakwater a small boat came up alongside the ship to take the pilot off. When I bade him good-bye I felt as though I was parting with an old friend. I noticed them bringing a very seedy looking character from the steerage. They hustled him down the ladder into the boat with the pilot, and then threw his old shoes and bundle in after him. He was what they call a stowaway. A look of disappointment crept over his face as they pulled away for the pilot boat, lying off in the distance. At 7:15 we passed out to sea. We ran beyond the reach of the storm in a short time. Soon the last vestige of land had disappeared, and we were speeding our way across the trackless ocean. I prepared myself for whatever demand Old " Neptune " might make upon me, but, to my surprise, he gave me the go-by. I seated myself on deck with my friends, thinking, after all, I might prove to be more seaworthy than I anticipated. I had my autoharp with me, and gave them a few selections, such as " Home, Sweet Home." It was quite in harmony with their feelings, as well as my own. Some one finally suggested that we adjourn to the saloon and have some singing. It was agreed to. Miss D—— presided at the piano. We sang some familiar pieces, the entire company joining. Mr. M—— has a fine voice, and gave us some excellent selections. I lost sight of the fact I was fast leaving America in the distance. They all expressed themselves as having spent the evening very pleasantly. That was the beginning of good times on the ship. I retired at 10:30, committing myself to the care of Him "who holds the great deep in the hollow of His hand."

FRIDAY, May 25.—I was awakened at 4 A. M. by voices pitched in a very high key. I listened, and presently I understood one of the lads to say: "Ye'er a liar!" I thought, now we are about to have the monotony of ship life broken by a free fight. I waited to learn what the result of an assertion like that would be. In a few moments a son of the Emerald Isle lifted up his voice and shouted: "Lift them higher." Then I understood what it meant. They were lifting the ashes from the hold of the ship, and instead of it being "ye'er a liar," it was "lift the bucket higher." I laid down in peace and slept until 6:30, when I found the ship rolling considerably, and it had a tendency to take the edge off my appetite. However, when the gong sounded the invitation for the morning meal, I entered the saloon with the faithful few. But my stay was very brief. "Neptune" had at last found me out, and demanded a settlement at once. I reluctantly gave up all the stock I had on hand. After this business transaction with the old gent, I decided not to lay in another supply for the present. I concluded to try a little poetry. I had a copy of Whittier's poems with me, and I suggested to Dr. R—— that we find some quiet place and spend a little time with the grand old Quaker poet, which we did, until the call came for dinner. The doctor obeyed the summons cheerfully, but I slowly wended my way to the dining-room. I did my best to relieve the table of its burden, but, when I had finished my first course, concluded to adjourn, to meet there again under more favorable circumstances. The doctor finally joined me again, and we resumed our reading. Suddenly things began to be rather prosy with me. I excused myself, and went on the double-quick to the side of the ship, and, as I gazed down into the dark blue sea, I wondered when I would see the last of that first course. That was the last time during the voyage that I was called on for a contribution. I became acquainted with many more of the passengers, among the number a very excellent man and his wife and daughter from Peoria, Ill. He, with quite a number of others, was returning to the home of his childhood on a visit. After tea we assembled on deck and spent the time in singing and pleasant conversation, until I almost lost sight of the fact I was on the broad Atlantic, whose bosom had been swept by the storms of ages. Some one discovered the lights of a ship far away in the distance. As it drew near our ship signalled her, and she displayed her friendly light, which we watched with a great deal of interest. Soon she disappeared. Some one quoted, very appropriately: "The ships that pass in the night." We had some fine talent on board. They were arranging for a concert to be given on the evening of Decoration Day.

SATURDAY, May 26.—When I came out on deck I felt better able to meet the day than I did the morning previous. I managed to adjust my sea legs so that I kept step a trifle better. We amused ourselves with various games and with the usual promenade on deck. I styled it the boardwalk. I began to enjoy "life on the ocean wave." I engaged in conversation with a very interesting lad who was travelling alone. He was on his way to Antwerp to join his father and mother. It was quite an undertaking for one so young, but he seemed equal to it. We had with us a Dr. C——, of Harrisburg, Pa., who, by his kind, genial manner, soon won the respect of all the passengers. He was going to Dublin to attend the Medical Convention. One of the gentlemen who was in company with him was a delegate to the World's Convention of the Y. M. C. A., held at Exerter Hall, London, commencing June 2nd, and closing on the 8th. I had the honor of being a delegate from our Association, Camden, N. J., to that wonderful Convention, but was not able to reach there until the 6th, as our ship was late in getting into port, and I was obliged to go to Harborn, near Birmingham, before going to London. Four sailing vessels passed during the day. We were all glad to see some life outside of our ship, on Old Ocean's dreary waste. There is always some excitement when anyone discovers a ship. The news spreads as rapidly as gossip in a little village. I saw a number of persons running to the forward part of the ship, and I understood one of them to say: "There is 'fire." I thought, is it possible that I have come out here to be cremated! I hurried to where the crowd had gathered, and learned the cause of the excitement. A school of porpoises were performing their gymnastics. I said to an Irish gentleman: "I thought some one said there was fire?" "And I did, too, sir," he replied. "And what would you have done if such had been the case?" I asked. "Sure, there's no chance to run; I should have stood and took it," he replied. I was requested to take part in the coming concert, but declined, for I had a very vivid recollection of my first, and it was also my last, appearance on the stage at a public entertainment. I was a small boy, but my conviction was, whatever my mission might be in this world, surely that was not my calling, and there had been no change in my mind.

SUNDAY, May 27.—I peeped out the porthole of my stateroom and discovered some very threatening-looking clouds skirting the horizon. I concluded that I should know what a storm at sea meant before the day had passed, but the rain came without the tempest, for which I was truly thankful. We were nearly in mid-ocean, but had not run beyond the Sabbath. The spirit of the day seemed to pervade the ship. The vast majority of the passengers were in the habit of observing the Lord's day, and even those who seemed inclined to forget their responsibility to their Creator were thoughtful, and felt the sacredness of the day. At 10:30 quite a large congregation gathered in the saloon for divine worship, the captain having charge. Miss M—— was to preside at the piano, but was sick, so they insisted on me filling the position, and also leading the singing. As I am not a professional I declined in favor of some one else, but they finally pressed me into service. The captain read the Episcopal service, and I led the singing in good, old-fashioned Methodistic style. I remarked to some of them that we had had a Methodist *Episcopal* meeting. The hymns we sang were: "Jesus, Lover of my Soul," and "Rock of Ages." I had sung them from my childhood, but they never seemed so sweet, or to contain so much meaning as they did that Sabbath, far, far out at sea. In the afternoon I perused the Bible, that old chart and compass which has guided so many storm-tossed mariners over the ocean of life, safe into the heavenly port. They had but one regular service on board, so after tea quite a number of us gathered in the saloon and held a song service. I think most of us, as we left the saloon and returned to our state-rooms, felt that the Sabbath spent out in mid-ocean had been a very profitable one.

MONDAY, May 28.—One would suppose we had an ample supply of water to tide us over, but it seemed not, for the clouds dropped down great sheets of it all the morning. I said to a gentleman formerly from the Green Isle: "This is a great body of water." "Sure, it is," he replied. I said: "I suppose if we had had anything to do with making this old world we would have fixed things different." "Sure, 'n we would have done with a few quarts less of water." We were deprived of the pleasure of being on deck, but with such excellent company one could be entertained wherever they were gathered. Among the leading ones who seemed bent on making things pleasant for us was a Mr. Geo. D——, of Germantown, Pa. He was what the Scotch people call "a cheery chap." He had a way of scattering sunshine that few men possess, and it was appreciated by the entire company. Mr. D——'s mother was traveling with him. She was a fine old Scotch lady. They were returning to their old home in Aberdeen, Scotland, for a visit. After the storm abated, Dr. R—— and I took a walk through the steerage. A large number of the steerage passengers were returning to their native land—on account of the depression of business in America. I do not often comment on the ladies' headgear, but a tall, gaunt-looking woman wore a bonnet that attracted my attention. It was either the very latest style, or dated back to the beginning of the century. It was built of straw, something in the shape of an old-fashioned covered wagon; it had an overcoming frill running around the entrance, and a cape with no lack of material. It did not strike the fancy of any of the ladies sufficiently for them to adopt the style. We ran into a dense fog early in the afternoon. The fog horn sounded rather doleful. It suggested to us there was a possibility of colliding with some stray craft, and of being compelled to exchange our comfortable quarters for a home down with the fish. The mist disappeared in a short time, and we had a beautiful sunset. It resembled a ball of fire, and seemed to drop into the ocean. I almost expected to hear the hissing sound that a ball of fire would produce falling into the water. I did not often see the sun rise. It was generally up attending to business before I found my way on deck. In the evening we were entertained by a Miss M———. She gave us several fine solos. She was on her way to London to finish her musical education. So closed our fourth day at sea.

TUESDAY, May 29.—The sun failed to put in its appearance. It was off duty most part of the time during our voyage. The clouds seemed to have the right of way. They looked as though they were getting ready to create a disturbance, and I felt that I would rather not see a *row* between the elements, for I knew we would be drawn into it. I watched with a great deal of interest the result of taking the log, and when the figures appeared on the board showing the distance we had traveled, I found we were in mid-ocean. I could scarcely realize that fifteen hundred miles of water swept between me and my dear old home. I was wonderfully impressed with the vastness of the Atlantic. One may stand on the shore and look out over the vast expanse of water and think it means something to cross to the other side, but he can have only a faint conception of what an undertaking it is. I felt as though all the world had been blotted out, and we were a small world, afloat on a wilderness of water. Those who were to take part in the concert of the next evening spent the morning practicing. We all looked forward to the entertainment with as much pleasure as a boy does when there is a circus coming to town. In the evening the sailors gathered on deck in front of their quarters, and two of them had musical instruments They played pieces that seemed to run down into the feet of some of the sailor lads. They began waltzing, and kept it up quite a while, much to the amusement of a number of the passengers.

WEDNESDAY, May 30.—I was awakened some time during the night by the howling of the wind and the violent tossing of the ship. I saw a pair of feet going up toward the top of the berth. At once I recognized them as my property. When I was a boy I frequently tried to stand on my head, but never succeeded very well. But I found myself performing the *feat* very gracefully this time. For some time after my advent into this old world, I am told, they rocked me to sleep in an old-fashioned cradle; but that was so long ago that I had become unaccustomed to that way of sleeping. I found being "rocked in the cradle of the deep" had a tendency to *disturb* my slumbers. Old Ocean was in a bad temper, and continued so all day. The water at times was piled up around us like a huge wall. It being Decoration Day, and also the evening for our concert, most of the day was spent in preparing for it. The saloon was trimmed very tastefully with flags. Over the piano the Stars and Stripes and the flag of old England were festooned. I was glad to see them blending so harmoniously. I understand it was not always the case; that back in the far distant past the Old Lady and her son, U. S. A., failed to agree on a certain question. She sought to bring him to terms, but he objected to the *rod*, and carried his point. But long before my recollection they became reconciled, and have been on friendly terms ever since. We remembered that it was the day when the graves of many of the brave soldiers would be strewn with flowers, and, although remembering that we were nearly two thousand miles from the land where sleeps their dust, and that we would not have the privilege of joining the multitude in placing the small tribute of remembrance on their graves, yet we knew that upon the wings of thought we could carry the flowers of respect and gratitude, and leave them there as our tribute. The concert commenced at 7.30, and the saloon was crowded. They had arranged a very good program, and it was well executed. Mr. Arthur M—— and a gentleman from Philadelphia sang a very appropriate piece, entitled, "Ship Ahoy." Judging from the heavy encore, the audience enjoyed it immensely. Mr. T——, of Philadelphia, gave a recitation, which was appreciated very much. "The Star Spangled Banner" and "God Save the Queen" were sung, the entire audience joining. The talent did themselves great credit. The admittance fee was a shilling, and the programs sold for a sixpence, so that quite a nice little sum was realized. The proceeds were given to the Liverpool Sailors' Orphanage, a very worthy institution. All expressed themselves as being delighted with the entertainment, and gave a vote of thanks to the committee.

THURSDAY, May 31.—The elements behaved as badly as on the night previous. They seemed to wreak vengeance on our craft, tossing her about regardless of our comfort. But she was well fastened together, and equal to all the pounding she received. She pushed her way along, bent on taking us safely to Liverpool. When I came out on deck I found it rather hard to manipulate my number nines. There was an old Yorkshireman rooming with George D——. He had a large vein of humor running through him, and greatly amused us. On leaving home, his wife (or old woman, as he styled her,) gave him a remedy for seasickness. The old gentleman failed to take it according to directions. He was decidedly "old school" in the quantity he used. We styled him Doctor, because he was always insisting on prescribing this same remedy for us. But, after listening to his description of it, we thought seasickness preferable. We did not see a friendly sail during the day. One would think, from the vast number of vessels that cross the Atlantic, we would have sighted more of them. I spent the evening in the saloon with a number of friends, retiring at 10:30. It was still storming.

FRIDAY, June 1.—When I awoke, I was surprised to find the sun had resumed business, after an absence of several days. We all greeted it with as much pleasure as we would had we met an old friend. The ocean had quite recovered from her fit of anger and was so calm and serene that it would seem impossible for her to get into such a bad temper as she had been in for several days past. Every one seemed cheerful and happy. Those who had been conspicuous by their absence at the table were at their post, and gave promise of making up for lost time. This was the tenth day out. Our ship's company had become almost like one family. Friendships were formed that I presume will be lasting. I am not quite sure that any of our young men met any one that they decided to take as a life partner, although some of them were quite interested. One in particular, I think, would have been quite willing to have had the voyage protracted, as reaching land meant separation. A lad who had a harmonica with him began to play some lively airs. Mr. A. M—— suggested that they have a waltz, and in a few moments quite a number were having a grand hop. I was invited to take part, but my education had been neglected along that line. They had a grand ball on deck in the evening. Two of the sailors furnished the music. There must have been a general overhauling of trunks, for the ladies and gentlemen came out tastefully attired for the occasion. While they were exercising themselves, I wrote letters home, expecting to mail them at Queenstown harbor.

SATURDAY, June 2.—Another beautiful day greeted us. I finished writing two little poems; one on my "Home Across the Sea," and another on "The Southwark." We sighted quite a number of vessels coming out from port. The topic of conversation was, "When shall we reach Queenstown?" The captain said he thought we would arrive there early Sunday morning. We were all anxious to see land. Some arranged to be on deck very early in the morning. Quite a number of the passengers were to land at Queenstown. Among the number was Dr. C—— and the two gentlemen traveling with him. I learned that Dr. C—— was one of the most prominent physicians of Harrisburg, Pa. We all felt as though we would rather not have our circle broken until we reached Liverpool. Several friends came to the Bachelor's Sanctum and spent the evening with me. When I bade them good night, I promised to meet them on deck early in the morning to hail the first sight of land.

SUNDAY, June 3.—I was awakened very early by the sound of footsteps on deck. I hurried out of my berth and looked out of the porthole, expecting to catch a glimpse of the Emerald Isle (not knowing I was on the wrong side of the ship to see land), but saw nothing but sky and water, and concluded we were still out at sea. While I was debating whether or not to climb back into my berth, the pin holding the deadlight came down on my head with such force as to make me think I must be near the land of shellalahs.

This encounter with the pin settled the question of the second edition of sleep. I decided to go on deck. When I did so, I found we were steaming up the Queenstown harbor. It is said to be one of the finest in the world. I shall never be able to describe my feelings as I looked out over the beautiful green fields of Old Ireland, stretching out from the brow of those bold sea cliffs, far away in the distance. There seemed to be such a variety of green. The farm-houses dotted over that fine stretch of country, with hedge rows surrounding them, had a fine effect. We all appreciated the sight of land after so many days on the briny deep. One old man excited the sympathy of those around him. As he stood and looked out over his native country, the tears ran down his wrinkled cheeks and he said : " Fifty years ago I left you ; would that I had never done so. I had eighteen uncles and aunts, and a number of other relatives when I left ; now I shall find the most of them sleeping in the old churchyard." His wife called him a baby, and told him to hush, but the old man continued to give expression to his feelings. We ran up the harbor within sight of Queenstown and dropped anchor. By the aid of field glasses I had a good view of the city. It was built on the side of a beautiful hill. I noticed some very fine residences. Just after we anchored, the Campania came up the harbor to take on passengers and the mail for America. She carried my first epistles from a foreign land to friends far away. It did not seem like the Sabbath day, the sailors busy lifting the luggage from the hold, and the passengers hurrying to and fro, making preparations to leave when the tender came out to us. When the strange-looking little craft came up alongside of our ship there was a general hand-shaking, and regrets expressed at having to part with those who did what they could to make the voyage a pleasant one. Soon they were on their way to Queenstown, and we sailed out of the harbor for Liverpool. When the shades of night crept on a heavy fog settled down upon us. Our steamer moved cautiously up the St. George's Channel. The fog horn sounded its notes of warning all through the night. We had no service in the morning, but in the evening several of us assembled in the saloon and held a song service. We were all anxious for the morning to dawn, for that meant getting on terra firma.

MONDAY, June 4.—When I came out on deck we were making our way up the river Mersey, and were within a short distance of Liverpool. We had an early breakfast and began preparing to land. It reminded me of moving day in New Jersey. We were interested to know whether the steamer would go direct to the docks, and thus avoid the unpleasantness of being transferred in the tender, for the wind was blowing a gale, and we were being treated to a drenching rain. But soon they dropped anchor, and we were informed that the steamer would not land us at the dock. After waiting quite a while for transportation, we heard a noise that sounded like the roar of some ferocious beast; as it drew near we found it was the whistle of the odd-looking boat called the tender. We were transferred to this uninviting looking craft, our only protection from the storm being a small awning. As we huddled together I said: "I am reminded of chickens taking refuge under an old hen." I thought several times the wind would carry away what little shelter we had. Several of the ropes holding it gave way. I tied one of them fast and said to "Doctor," our Yorkshire friend, "Attend the main sheet, will you?" He replied in his broad Yorkshire dialect, "I'm no boatswain; I paid my passage; I'll not lay a hand's turn to it." This reply quite amused us, as well as some others he made during the short but uncomfortable trip from the ship to the Princess Landing. I felt like bounding up in the air a few feet when I stepped on *terra firma*. We had our baggage taken to the custom house, a large building on the wharf. It was nicely arranged, so that they have very little trouble in examining luggage. There are benches extending across the building; everything is placed on them, and an excellent corps of men, who quite understand their business, soon examined everything. I had two small satchels, and a telescope filled with books entitled, "Songs From Bethany," which I published the year previous, a number of the songs being my own composition. One of them, entitled, "Saves a Sinner Like Me," I afterward found them singing all over England, Ireland and Scotland. They requested me to open my satchels, and then looked into them. They asked me whether or not I had any spirits or tobacco concealed in them. I said, "No." I thought if they had known what an experience I had when a boy with tobacco, they would not have asked that question, and the little old "brown jug" and I were not on good terms by any means. They inquired what I had in the telescope. I informed them. My luggage was then marked O. K., and I had it sent to Lime Street Station with that of friend A. M—— and Mrs. D——.

On the Shores of Old England

DOCTOR R—— and I sallied forth to see the city, promising to meet our friends at the station in time for the train leaving at 4 P. M. I was quite surprised to find such a large city, and to see so many fine business houses. The streets were thronged with people hurrying to and fro, just as eager for the "filthy lucre" as the Americans. The city has quite a river front, and the docks are a sight worth seeing. We found some difficulty in understanding the money. "One-and-six," "Two-pence," "Ha'-penny," etc., were Greek to us. I said to the Doctor, "when we purchase anything we will give them a large piece of money and trust to their honesty in giving us the correct change." I soon became accustomed to it, and managed it very nicely. We called at the Y. M. C. A. hall, and met with a very cordial reception from the assistant secretary. We were shown through the building, which is a very fine one. I said, "God bless those who have given their time and money for an institution of this kind, which has been the means of saving a great many men from being wrecked by the saloon." Quite a number of young men were availing themselves of its privileges. There are quite a number of places of interest in Liverpool. So many make a mistake in not spending a few days there. I purposed stopping a short time prior to leaving for home. We left on the 4 P. M. train. It seemed very strange, riding in one of those English carriages. They are divided into five compartments. The doors open on the side, and the seats face each other. Each seat holds five persons. As a rule they lock the door of the carriage when the train leaves the station. The scenery from Liverpool to Birmingham is very picturesque. I enjoyed the ride. We passed through quite a number of tunnels. Mr. M—— and family, the D—— family, and Dr. R—— left me at Derby. They took the train for Nottingham. Mr. T—— and wife were going to Birmingham, and I was very glad of it. We arrived at New Street Station at 7:50. It is said to be the largest railway station in the world. It seemed to be an immense affair to me that eve. Mr. T—— kindly showed me the way to New street, where I was to take the 'bus for Harborn, a suburban town two miles distant. When I bade him adieu, I was alone in a strange land. I got two street arabs to carry my luggage to the starting point of the 'bus, a short distance up the street. I saw them watching me with a great deal of curiosity, and I said to one of them: "Where do you think I am from?" He said: "Ye'r from London." I turned to the other boy and said: "And where do you say I am from?" He scanned me very closely and said: "Ye'r from Ireland." I had been told before leaving home that I would pass for a native of the Emerald Isle. I said: "No, I am from America." They opened their eyes wide and said: "Oh, I'd like to go there." I rode on the top of the 'bus through some of the principal streets, and concluded I was in no mean city. It was very American-like in its appearance. The city is built up nearly to Harborn with very beautiful residences. Harborn is situated on a hill overlooking a grand stretch of country, and is a neat, pretty suburban town. It contains a number of elegant residences, most of them being the homes of prominent business men of Birmingham. It is the native town of my friend, Fred P——, now living in New York, a young man whom I have been interested in ever since he came to our shores. He was very anxious I should visit his old home. His father and mother sent me a very cordial invitation to come and make their home my headquarters during my sojourn in that country. I had some gifts for them from their boy in America, and also desired to leave the bulk of my books with them until I was ready to go to South Littleton, in Worcestershire, and to the adjoining shire, where I expected to dispose of them. I therefore thought it best to go directly to their home, even though it would make me very late in getting to the Convention in London. I never shall forget the kind reception they gave me when I entered their home. One would have thought I was a member of the household returning, instead of the tall stranger from America. I at once felt I was in the hands of genuine friends, and never had the slightest cause to change my mind. I found them to be refined, intelligent people, and very highly respected in the community in which they lived. The family at home consisted of two sons and two daughters. One of the sons, a very bright, genial young man, graduated in pharmacy during my stay. The other son was an interesting boy of eleven years. One of the daughters was an accomplished young lady, one who could entertain you at the piano, and also had a practical knowledge of domestic duties. The other daughter was a very bright little girl of about thirteen summers, and one of the most original characters that I have met with. I also met with a Mr. S—— F——, a fine fellow, holding a good position in one of the banks. He was paying attention to the young lady, with a fair prospect of some time becoming a member of the family. We had supper about 10 o'clock. I wondered how I was to manage four meals a day, especially roast beef and all the fixings, at so late an hour, but soon became accustomed to it, and enjoyed it as much as a full-fledged Englishman. They remarked I did not talk like an American. All the Americans they had met with said, with a nasal twang, "I guess" and "calculate." I began to think about the boy's remarks in reference to my coming from Ireland, and they expressing themselves as they did, possibly I would not be as much of a stranger as I anticipated. I was very much pleased and interested in the affectionate manner in which they bade each other good night. I admired their home life, and wished all the homes the world over were conducted in like manner.

TUESDAY, June 5.—When I awoke the birds were having a grand concert near my window; not the monotonous twittering of sparrows, but birds that could strike notes with some music in them. I quite enjoyed their songs. I saw comparatively few sparrows. I concluded they had emigrated to America, where we would only be too glad to bid them farewell, and see them "homeward fly." On the opposite side of the street stands the Old Harborn Church. It is on an elevation of about three feet above the street, with a beautiful shaded yard surrounding it, where sleep the dead of many centuries. Mr. P—— informed me that there had been a church there for more than eight hundred years. The present church was rebuilt during the present century, but the tower was the original one built in King John's time. I have always had a fondness for antiquity, and I expressed a desire to go through the church. He is a prominent member of it, and was only too glad to show me through. A feeling of awe crept over me as I climbed those old stone steps, worn by the press of many feet during the past eight hundred years. When I reached the top, where hang the chimes, some of which have been in use for a great number of years, I thought, how often have they rung out their glad anthems on festive occasions, and tolled the solemn dirge as friends were slowly following some loved one to his quiet resting place in the old churchyard. I copied from a tablet in the church, near the altar, the name of Rev. Edward Roberts, one of the rectors of recent years. One of the inscriptions read: "He left a host of friends when he passed to the glory land." I was very much impressed with the one at the base of the tablet: "He spent his whole life in promoting the spiritual and temporal welfare of his fellow men." What a grand record to leave! More enduring than a huge marble shaft. I heard him spoken of as a man who possessed the true spirit of Christ, his Master. After looking through that old edifice, that seemed sacred to me, we went through the "silent city of the dead." While there Mr. Walter

C——'s head gardener came in. He was a good-natured looking man, possessed with a large vein of humor. Mr. P—— introduced me as Fred's friend, from America. He said, with a merry twinkle in his eye and a smile playing over his face, "Ah, indeed; so you came from the land where they could only boast of one man that never told a lie." I was quite amused at the way he spoke of the "Father of our Country." He had evidently read the history of little George and the hatchet. I said to him, "You are putting the rest of us back in the shade." I was interested in reading some of the epitaphs on the time-worn tombstones. I copied the following one:

"Here lies beneath this mouldering sod,
An honest man, the noblest work of God;
A father kind, a husband dear;
Such was the man that lies slumbering here."

They pointed out a very odd one. A woman had buried three husbands, and she was not ashamed to let the world know that she had gone to the parson's on a matrimonial errand so many times, for she had all three of their names on one stone. I smiled when I read the epitaph. It was as follows:

"This turf has drunk a widow's tears;
Three of her husbands slumber here."

Our portly, humorous friend invited us to his house. It was formerly the rectory of the church. It was more than two hundred years old. It was built of stone and was very quaint, especially the interior. He also showed us through the grounds of Mr. Walter C——'s elegant mansion. They were tastefully arranged. I don't think I ever saw any finer. The greenhouses, as well as the grounds, contained flowers and plants from nearly all parts of the world. It was quite interesting to hear our friend describe the different species. I saw a piece of surgery that he did. They had a pet stork that in some way injured its leg so that amputation was necessary. He was equal to the emergency, and performed a skilful operation, and had also made an artificial leg for the unfortunate bird. I was greatly amused, when he gave a shrill whistle, to see it come bounding to him, putting the wooden leg down as though it meant business. It seemed to appreciate the wooden prop. I was afterward shown through some parts of this beautiful home. It was neatly but richly furnished. In the reception-room was an open stairway, at the base of which were two pieces of elegant statuary. There was a broad landing half way up, nicely arranged. The smoking- and billiard-rooms lacked nothing along that line. There was a miniature museum containing curiosities from nearly all parts of the world. I noticed some old Indian relics from America. Mr. C—— has traveled extensively. There is a private electric plant on the grounds. It is a home that lacks nothing that money can purchase to make it comfortable. Mr. C—— is a brother to Mr. R. C——, one of England's most illustrious statesmen. In the afternoon I went to Birmingham. I got off the 'bus at the Five Ways, walked down Great Colmore street, and called at a home and gladdened the heart of the lady by good tidings and gifts from dear ones in America. I then found my way through the busy streets to the Y. M. C. A. hall.

The secretary was at the Convention, but I met the assistant, a young man well qualified for the position. I introduced myself to him, and he at once made me feel at home. We had quite a protracted conversation on the work in England and America. They have a large hall, but it is poorly located. It is in Nedless alley, a small thoroughfare running off New street. New street is one of the principal business streets, and contains a number of large stores. I enjoyed the ride on the top of the 'bus back to Harborn. I engaged in conversation with an interesting old gentleman. He thought I came from Derbyshire. I began to think I must be a decided mixture. In the evening Mr. P—— took me to the Harborn Free Reading-Room. They have a fine library and periodicals of all kinds. There was no excuse for any man in that vicinity not storing his mind with good reading matter. We passed the Salvation Army barracks, and heard them singing lustily. I suggested we stop for a few minutes, and we did so, and heard a remarkable experience given by a young lady recently converted. She was very intelligent, and expressed herself so. When we returned home I was quite ready for the fourth meal. I much enjoyed gathering around the family board, not simply for the delicious food set before me, but for the good social time. Mrs. P——'s refined wit I shall not soon forget.

My First Night in London.

WEDNESDAY, June 6.—I arose early and began making preparations for my trip to London. I confess I was rather loth to leave the friends who had shown me so much kindness. They assured me a welcome awaited me whenever I chose to come to my "English home." I went to Birmingham and took the 10 A. M. express. The guard, as they call him, examined our tickets before leaving the station, then locked us in, and we were soon speeding along at a rapid rate through another beautiful part of the country. We stopped only at the principal towns. At Northampton a fine looking gentleman and lady boarded the train. They came into the same compartment I was in, she taking a seat beside me, he seating himself by the window opposite me. I offered to exchange seats with him so that they could be together, but he thanked me very politely, and assured me he was not particular about changing. They carried on a pleasant conversation with each other for a little while, then he became absorbed in the daily paper. Presently he passed the paper to her, calling her attention to an article that had pleased him very much, and I laid aside my better training and cast a side glance at the article, and saw it was something in reference to the Y. M. C. A. Convention. Immediately I began to lay a plan to form his acquaintance, which I did by asking what time the train was due in London. He very readily gave me the information, and asked me if I knew anything about London. I said: "No; I have only been in England two days; I am a delegate from America to the Y. M. C. A. Convention." "Ah, indeed," he replied; "I am a delegate from our Association at Northampton, and my wife and I are going direct to the Convention, and as you are a stranger and know nothing about the city, you are entirely welcome to go with us to the hall." I thanked him kindly, and in reply said I did not care to intrude on them in any way. They both replied: "Not at all; we would only be too glad to have you go with us." I concluded I had fallen into the hands of good friends, and thought no further invitation was necessary. He gave me a very glowing account of the Convention, as he had been there nearly every day. I quite regretted that I had not been able to meet with them at the commencement. When we arrived at the Euston Square Station he secured a hack, and we were driven to Exeter Hall. He said to me: "This is Jubilee Day, and as the Secretary is busy and you may have some trouble in getting your credentials through, just give them to me, and I think I can manage them for you." So he left his wife and me in the reading-room, and in a short time returned, saying that he had gotten everything but my ticket for the Jubilee Concert and the book containing my checks for dinner, but would secure them if possible. I begged him not to go to any further trouble, as I had already taken too much of his valuable time, and also deprived his wife of his company. She said: "It is a pleasure for me to have my husband do anything he can for you. If we should come to America, we would expect the same kind of treatment." " Indeed," I replied, " there will be one tall American that will see that you receive it, if it be within his power." Presently he returned with a ticket for the entertainment at the Albert Memorial Hall, but the check-books for dinner had all been given out. However, he said, he had an extra check that he thought I could use. They had erected a temporary pavilion on the Thames embankment, seating comfortably 2,300 persons, and in it dinner was served for the delegates during the Convention. His wife took dinner at the restaurant connected with Exeter Hall, and we went to the pavilion. It was a fine sight to see that grand body of Christian men, representing nearly every country in the world, partaking of dinner together. The tables were nicely arranged, laden with tempting food, and the tall Yankee was not long in demonstrating to those around him how much he appreciated that noon-day meal. There were syphons filled with various kinds of soft drinks. Mr. J——, my newly found friend, helped me to a glass of lemonade, and when I was ready for the second edition I thought I could manipulate the syphon without troubling him. I pressed a little too hard, and instead of me getting the cooling draught, a lady sitting opposite had it sprinkled profusely over her new gown. I was chagrined, and in a confused manner begged her pardon. She made no reply, but gave me a look that had no forgiveness in it. That withering look affected my appetite some little, but I recovered it sufficiently to manage the rest of the courses.

When we returned to Exeter Hall, Sir George Williams, whom the Queen had recently knighted, was giving a reception to the delegates. The hall was densely packed, but we managed to find seats on the platform. There was a certain number of delegates appointed from each country on the reception committee. Sir George stood there with his face beaming with the light of our holy Christianity. The delegates came from China, Japan, India, the islands of the sea, from the frozen North, and from other countries far and near. Each committee bore some gift as a slight token of love and esteem for this venerable man who had been such a great blessing to the world. I thought, as he received those kind remembrances, what must be his feelings? There must have been one grand doxology going up from his heart to the Triune God for dropping into his mind the thought of gathering those few young men into that small room at No. 72 St. Paul's Churchyard, London, to talk and pray about more effectual work for their divine Master. That little meeting, held fifty years ago, was the nucleus of the Young Men's Christian Association. It has deepened and widened until to-day, from North to South, from East to West, the Y. M. C. A. boys, with hearts filled with the same strong love for Christ and His cause that characterized those noble young men of a half century ago, are still stretching out their hands and rescuing those who, but for their effort, might be eternally lost. There was a ripple of laughter passed over the audience when Mr. B., one of the representatives of Old Ireland, made his speech, and presented the gift. He apologized for the lateness in getting to the meeting, saying it was " owing to the indisposition of the Irish Sea." He was well laden with wit. When the neat, trim little Japanese came upon the platform to express the good wishes of the young men of his far-away country, the audience all turned Methodist, and shouted and waved their handkerchiefs, rejoicing in the great fact that in lands where idolatry seemed to predominate, young men had been saved by the power of Christ, and were banded together to hold up the light of the gospel amid the gross darkness of those countries. The hymns they used were written in several different languages. They sang that old, inspiring hymn,

>"Blest be the tie that binds
>Our hearts in Christian love."

I thought as I heard that vast audience joining in that sweet song, what but the religion of Jesus could thus cement hearts together? I shall carry the sweet remembrance of that wonderful meeting with me all through my pilgrimage. Mr. J―― said to me: " I shall have to go with my wife on some business, and return home on the 5 P. M. train, but before I go, I will leave a note with the assistant secretary, for a gentleman in my employ, whom I am expecting here in a short time. He is coming down to attend the grand jubilee concert this evening, and as he is comparatively a stranger in London, and you have not as yet secured permanant quarters, I would like you to meet him and stop at the same hotel." Thus it was arranged that I should be notified by the secretary of the arrival of this gentleman. Just as they were leaving the hall, their two sons came in ; one of them about sixteen years old, the other, nineteen. I was introduced to them and found them bright, clean-cut lads. When I bade Mr. J—— and wife good bye, I said to them: "You have built a monument of kind deeds to-day, that I shall never take down." While I was waiting for the gentleman to put in an appearance, Mr. J—— unexpectedly came back, and was quite disappointed in finding that his friend had not arrived, but just as he was about to leave, he and two of his friends came in. I was introduced to them, and Mr. J—— informed him of his plan. He very readily assented to it. They were good, sociable fellows, and made me feel at home in their presence at once. After tea, we went to Charing Cross Station, and took the train by the underground railway for South Kensington, where the Albert Memorial Hall is situated. Our tickets were for different parts of the hall, so when we separated at the entrance, the understanding was we were to meet at Exeter Hall at the close of the entertainment. The usher informed me that my ticket called for a seat up toward the dome, so I began the journey. When I had climbed several flights of stairs and thought surely I had reached the place where I could rest my weary frame, I was informed there were still higher heights for me to attain. When there were no more stairways for me to ascend, I looked about for the seat that I thought my ticket entitled me to, and found it meant standing up. It is an immense circular hall, with a glass domed roof. The interior is 210 feet in diameter and 137 feet high. There are accommodations for 10,000 persons, the orchestra holding 1,000 performers. It was a grand sight, as I looked down from my lofty height. It was beautifully illuminated, and packed to its utmost capacity. The program was an excellent one: Organ recital, by Mr. Wm. Carter; reception of guests, by the President and by President of the Jubilee Council; selections of music, by a Swedish male voice choir, many of the singers being students of the Upsala University. Their sweet songs thrilled that vast audience. The encores were tremendous. The gymnastic display was very fine. It was under the direction of Mr. A. Alexander. They performed some feats that were marvelous. Then there was a selection of sacred music by Wm. Carter's choir. Madam Antoinett Stirling sang a beautiful solo; her voice seemed to fill every nook and corner of that large hall. There were addresses by some very prominent divines. The unveiling of the bust of Sir George Williams was very interesting. There was an exhibition of lime-light views, illustrating the rise and progress of the Young Men's Christian Association. I grew weary of having to stand, and found my way out and took a Strand coach, and went back to Exeter Hall. It was raining very hard, and I wondered whether or not the trio would think it best to come all the way back to the hall. I had my doubts about it. When I went into the reading-room there were two gentlemen sitting at a table, reading. I asked one of them if he had any objection to my joining the circle. He looked up with his face packed full of sunshine, and said pleasantly: "Not at all; be seated." We at once engaged in conversation. He informed me he was a delegate from Sterling, Scotland, and gave me his name as J. J——. I told him I was from America. A look of surprise crept over his face. He replied: "I thought you were a big Irishman from the north; why, you have the appearance of one." I replied: "I have had the same remark made before, sir." I told him I had not yet secured lodgings, and was expecting to go with three gentlemen when they returned from the entertainment. He urged me to go with him, for it was raining so hard he did not think they would come, and as it was the night of the Derby races, he thought it would be difficult for me to get a place, for the rooms of many of the hotels were engaged ahead on Derby night. I thanked him and told him I thought I had better wait for them. He invited me to visit him when I came to Scotland. A friendship sprang up between us that I believe will last through all time, and reach out in the great beyond. I began to get anxious about the return of my friends, especially when a little old man came hurrying into the hall, and, in an excited manner, asked the assistant secretary if he could tell him where he could get lodging. He had been to most of the hotels in that vicinity, he said, and found them full. The secretary said: "No; it is eleven o'clock, and rather late to look after that matter now." I told him that I was without hotel accommodations, and then gave him the reason. "I can only direct you to the Newington Causeway Y. M. C. A. hall, where they have lodging rooms," he replied; "you may possibly be accommodated there." He told me to go down the Strand to Waterloo Bridge, where I could take a coach direct to Newington Causeway. So I started out in the rain, and was like a ship at sea without chart or compass, in the streets of the great city of London. The streets were thronged with people of every description, most of them coming from the theatres in that locality. The omnibusses were packed. As I was going over the bridge I ventured to ask a young man if he could tell me whether I was going in the direction of Newington Causeway? He looked up through his eye-glasses, and in a very tart manner replied: "I don't know anything about it." I thought I had better pass on, or he might think I was after his pocketbook, instead of information. I plodded along, weary, wet, and a trifle blue. After I had walked a long distance an omnibus drove near the curb to let some one out. I hailed the driver and asked him if he went near Newington Causeway. He informed me that he did. I got in and told the chap to notify me on reaching there, and he did so. I stepped up to a policeman standing on the corner and asked him whether he could tell me where the Young Men's Christian Association hall was. "Whose place do you mean?" he asked; "Dunn's?" "Oh," I replied, "I don't know whether that is the name or not; I know I am about *done*." "That is the place, I think, you are looking for," pointing to a building on the opposite side of the street. I hurried across the street and pulled the bell. A young man came to the door, rubbing his eyes, apparently two-thirds asleep. I asked him if he could accommodate me with a bed. "No," he replied; "all full except one, and I am waiting for the young man to come in who is to occupy that; wish he'd come, I want to go to bed." I said to him, in a pleading tone of voice: "Can't you stow me away somewhere out of the storm?" I related to him how I happened to be without a shelter. "I can do nothing for you," he said, "as the matron has retired, and I do not care to disturb her." I inquired if he knew of a hotel near by? "No," he replied; "I have not been here long." "I have not, either," I said, "and never want to be again, under these circumstances," and bade him good night. I stepped out in the storm again, not knowing where I was going. Old "Big Ben," the huge clock at Westminster, had long since rung out the hour of twelve. I walked down the street as though I was familiar with the locality. I knew it was very rough by the characters I met, and I did not think it safe to make inquiry of any of them in reference to hotels. I walked a long way, until finally I met a policeman. I asked him if he could direct me to a hotel? "You are on the wrong side of the river for them," he said; "I do not know of one short of London Bridge." I was anxious to know the distance. "About a twenty minutes' walk," he informed me. I felt like dropping down on the curbstone and sleeping with one eye open. There were no coaches running on the street, and I was obliged to press my way on, though footsore and weary. My umbrella did its best to shelter me, but after so long a pelting by the merciless storm, it began to fail me. It seemed to me that I had been walking about an hour when I saw, under the electric light, a young man with a satchel in his hand, talking to a policeman. "There is some one as badly off as I am," I thought, so I crossed the street, and, as I approached them, heard the uniformed gentleman say to him: "I can't tell you; I have sent a number of men to both the Bridge and the Waverly hotels, and they have failed to get rooms. This is Derby night, that means all the hotels are filled; and then, as it is very late, I doubt whether you can find accommodations anywhere." Then I stepped up and said: "I am in the same fix; can't you tell me of some place where I can get in out of the storm. It is rather a trying position—here in the streets of this great city, at this hour, without any prospect of a refuge." I scanned the young man closely, and decided that he was a very respectable fellow. He had a very troubled look, and I am sure I had. I again appealed to the policeman to know whether he could not think of some place he could direct me to? "Oh, yes!" he said; "I do know of one just around here on Duke street, kept by an Italian." That struck terror to me. "They have a bad reputation over in our country," I said; "I have only a few coppers, and I do not care to lose them." "There is no danger of that," he replied. I asked the young man if he would go around with me? "Yes; let us go and see what it is like; we must have some place to stay," he replied. The blue-coated lad offered to take us, so we went with him. It was only a short distance, but I had a troop of thoughts going through my mind. One of them was: Possibly this policeman is in league with the Italian, and I am being led into a death-trap. I wondered whether I would ever see dear old America again, or whether I would be dispatched and cast into the Thames, which was flowing near by. When we reached "Hotel de Italia" the policeman pulled the bell. Presently I heard the sound of footsteps coming through the hall. The door was opened rather cautiously, and the proprietor of this, the only refuge that offered itself to us, stood there holding a penny dip in his hand, peeping out with an inquiring look. I cast my eyes into that long, dark hallway, and asked myself the question whether I had not better take my chances on the street. Our uniformed friend asked him if he could give us lodging? He said he could, and inquired whether we wanted to room together. I said, "No." I stepped into the hall and followed the man that I regarded with so much suspicion. I had not proceeded far before I discovered the young man had not come in. I hastened to the door, thinking surely I was in the hands of the Philistines. I found him in conversation with the policeman, and saw him give him a fee for bringing us around. So I stepped out and followed suit. Then we went in and took up the line of march. I shall never forget that midnight parade: the Italian, with his little, flickering torch, on the lead, and the tall American—his only weapon an umbrella—and the little Englishman, with his carpet-bag, bringing up in the rear. As we climbed the stairway, I wondered under what circumstances I should come down, and my comrade, judging from his grave look, had thoughts similar to mine. We were ushered into a room on the second floor, which, to our surprise, was neatly furnished. Turning to my "partner in distress," the proprietor said: "This is your room." I bade him good night, and suspiciously followed my guide up another flight of stairs. I was shown into a fairly respectable room. He lighted the gas, and informed me that the charges were a half crown (about 62 cents in United States money). I was not long in settling my bill and getting him off my hands. I had all my money with me, so I concluded I had better stand guard, as in case I was attacked I would be better prepared to raise an objection to having company at so late an hour. I am not a belligerant character, but I resolved if the little Italian came along to demand my cash, I would lay hold of him and do my best to shake out of his head any idea he may have entertained of laying violent hands on my pocketbook. As I surveyed my room, my eyes rested on some small pictures in quaint old frames hanging on the wall. As I approached them I was greatly surprised to find them Bible scenes. One of them was Christ blessing the children; the others were similar. As I gazed on those simple little pictures my fears vanished as quickly as did those of the hunter who was lost in a forest one night, and was compelled to seek lodging at a little cabin. The occupants were rough, uncouth-looking persons, and he regarded them with suspicion, and concluded, like myself, to postpone sleeping until a more favorable opportunity. But when the old man read the family Bible, and he and his wife knelt in prayer, a feeling of security took possession of him, and he laid down and slept peacefully. And so I reasoned: If this man has such pictures in his home, he must, at least, respect the *old Book*, and may not be such a villian as I think him, and I may not, after all, be in a den of thieves, but in the home of a Christian. I reasoned myself out of my wet clothing into bed. It was something after two o'clock when I laid my weary frame down to rest, and was soon unconscious of the fact I was on the third floor of an Italian lodging house in the great city of London.

My Three Weeks in London.

THURSDAY, June 7.—When I awoke the storm clouds had disappeared and the sun was peeping in through the old-fashioned windows, seeming to congratulate me on getting through the eventful night safely. The delegates were to spend the day at Windsor Castle, as the closing exercises were to be held there. They were to go in sections. The one I was to go with left Paddington Station at 8 A. M. I had no idea where it was. I had to go to Exeter Hall before taking the train, and I knew I was a long distance away, judging from the tramp I had the night previous. I found I had no time to tarry in what proved to be a very comfortable bed. My clothing, which had been drenched during my wanderings in the storm, I had spread about the room, giving it the appearance of wash-day in "Shanty Town." Alas for me, I found them nearly as moist as when I retired. I questioned whether it would not be wiser for me to forego the pleasure of the trip to Windsor and remain where I was until the last vestige of pneumonia had evaporated from my mud-besprinkled garments, for I already had an intimation that handkerchiefs would be essential articles during the day, but I concluded to risk it. I soon found my way down from my lofty perch to the hallway. I saw no one about but a boy; he came from the dining-room, to let me out. I looked into the little dingy restaurant and concluded not to remain for breakfast, as it would consume too much time to wait for edge enough on my appetite to enjoy a meal there. When my feet touched the pavement, I felt like singing a song of praise for safe deliverance. I should have liked to have seen my comrade and congratulated him on seeing the light of another day, but my time was limited. I learned that only a short distance away I could take an omnibus direct to Exeter Hall. Nearly all of them, as well as the street cars, or trains as they are styled, have seats on top. I took one of the lofty seats and enjoyed the ride over the famous London bridge. I could scarcely realize I was passing over the old bridge that I had heard of from childhood. There is one continuous mass of people and vehicles pouring over it from early dawn until long after the shades of night have crept on. I had a grand view of the Thames. The embankment presented a fine appearance. As we rode through the crowded streets, I wondered how our driver could escape a collision, but he understood the art of driving through a very narrow space. I was directed by the secretary at the hall how to reach Paddington Station. Seated near me in the coach were two Germans; one of them wore a Y. M. C. A. badge, and was a delegate from an Association in the interior of Germany; he could not speak a word of English. The other one said to me in broken English: "This is a friend of mine; he is going to Windsor on that 8 A. M. train. If we miss it I don't know what I shall do with him, for I shall have to go back to my business, and he will not be able to get

4

along by himself." The horses moved very slowly; they seemed to feel the weight of years. I knew unless the driver applied his whip a little heavier than he was doing, we would not make it. Sure enough, just as we entered the station the train moved out with the delegates. I saw the trouble the man was in and said to him: "I think I understand enough of the German language to make this young man know he is in safe hands, so leave him in my charge." He thanked me and gladly resigned him to my care. I was informed by one of the guards that our tickets would be good on the train leaving an hour later. I soon passed out all the German that I knew and we had a good, quiet time afterward. The ride to Windsor was a very enjoyable one; we passed through some very pretty country. The view of Windsor Castle as we approached it, was very fine. The town of Windsor is about twenty-five miles from London. It contains a population of 12,000 people, including the two regiments of soldiers which are always quartered there. The Queen, for whom I have the most profound respect, believing her to be a grand, good Christian woman, granted the request of the committee to visit the Castle, Frogmore, the Royal Gardens, the Royal Mausoleum, the late Prince Consort's farm, and other places of interest, and also gave them permission to erect a large pavillion in the Home Park, where the entire company were served with a dinner that did great credit to the Committee. A short walk from the station brought my German responsibility and I to the wonderful Castle. Fortunately we met his section at the entrance. He gave me a warm shake of the hand, which indicated to me that his heart was full of gratitude for the little attention I had given him. I was intensely interested in the Albert Memorial Chapel. The policeman stood at the entrance and kept us on the move. I was so taken with the beauty of it, that I fell in line two or three times, and each time taxed my eyes to their utmost. History tells us it was originally built as a royal mausoleum by Henry VII., who, however, was buried at Westminster. It was once destroyed by a mob. After remaining in ruins for a hundred years, it was reconstructed as a royal mausoleum by George III. Queen Victoria has restored it in honor of the late Prince Consort. The chapel is 68 feet long, by 28 feet wide, and about 60 feet high. The interior of this chapel is said to be one of the finest in the world. It is made of very highly polished marbles. The gilt mosaics and the magnificent stained glass produce a fine effect. The walls contain "pictures in marble," depicting a series of Biblical subjects, Moses, Abraham, Daniel, and a number of others. In the chancel the subjects are Gethsemane, Calvary, and the Entombment. At the east end of the chapel is a recumbent figure of the Prince Consort; at the west end is a sarcophagus of the late Duke of Albany, in white marble; in the centre is a sarcophagus of the late Duke of Clarence, raised on marble steps, containing panels of Mexican onyx. It supports a recumbent figure of the Prince. He is said to have been a very promising young man, and the Queen mourns the loss of her grandson very much. I thought, as I lingered there for a few moments, surely Death is no respecter of persons; he enters the royal palace as well as the little hovel to claim his victims. I came out and passed through the Norman gateway leading to the State departments. The first room we entered was the Queen's audience chamber. It was hung with gobelin tapestry, representing the story of Queen Esther and Mordecai. The paintings on the ceiling were magnificent. The presence chamber was also hung with fine tapestry, representing a continuation of the story of Esther. It was made in the time of King Charles II. There were a table used at the coronation of King George IV., the cabinet of Louis XIV., and portrait of Mary, Queen of Scots, with the picture of her execution at the base of it, and the portrait of Queen Victoria, in this room. In the guard-room was the colossal bust of Nelson, on a pedestal cut out of the foremast of the old warship "Victory." There is a hole in this pedestal, made by a ball from the enemy's gun. The grand reception-room is said to be 90 feet long and 34 feet wide, hung with tapestry representing the story of Jason and Medea. I admired an immense vase, presented to the Queen by the Czar of Russia. The throne-room was decorated in blue, with a carved ivory throne, presented by a man with a name hard to manage, Maharajah, of Travanaco. It is a marvelous piece of work. Waterloo chamber, or grand dining-room, is 98 feet long, 47 feet wide and 45 feet high, and decorated in white and gold. I noticed portraits of a number of noted officers that took part in the great battle of Waterloo. The grand vestibule contains old armors and banners, some of them very ancient. Some of the Queen's jubilee presents were in this room. A number of them I recall vividly, one being a model of the Albert Memorial, in solid gold. There were also models of two warships in silver. These were gifts from Mahrajah of Johore. There was a fan of ostrich feathers, several feet high, with several smaller ones at each side, made of pea-fowls' feathers. It was a very artistic piece of work. There was a large silk curtain with a beautifully embroidered fowl on it; also one with a deer on, and another with a large crane. They were said to be emblems of longevity. There was also a block of carved jade on a pedestal of rosewood, symbolic of long life, stability and immutability. These were gifts from H. I. M., Emperor of China. I should like to devote more space to the description of this wonderful castle. It is said to be one of the largest and finest royal residences in the world. I visited the round tower, from which, in fine weather, it is said twelve counties can be seen. I had a grand view of the country. The Thames, winding through the meadows, was charming, and the town of Windsor presented a fine picture. I became acquainted with three Swedish young men; one of them was postmaster at Stockholm; the others were brothers and sons of a prominent professor. They were very bright, intelligent fellows, and spoke English fairly well. I went with them to the large tent and dined with them. On each side of me were Swedes, opposite were Norwegians; just below me was a Chinaman and a dusky son of India, and as I cast my eyes over that immense pavilion, I could see men representing nearly every nation on the globe. I found the Swedish folk very much interested in America, and I was as much so in hearing of their home in the frozen North. In coming out of the park from dinner I met a Mr. A—— from Dayton, Ohio. We took a walk through the town, which like most of the English towns, was kept in excellent order. I then went back to the castle. I stood at the door of the old St. George's Chapel and listened to some fine singing. I afterward went through this grand edifice. The great west window contains six tiers of compartments, each six feet in height. They contain seventy-five figures, including Edward the Confessor, several kings, knights and bishops. By going to dinner when I did, I missed the opportunity of a visit to Frogmore and to the royal gardens and royal farm. I regretted it very much, for I met a number of delegates who had been there, and they gave me a grand description of it. At a given time all the delegates were to assemble at the east terrace to be photographed. At the entrance leading into these beautiful grounds two men were stationed. They called out: "All foreign delegates please come this way to be photographed first." Mr. A—— and I fell into line, and were informed that we were not foreign delegates. We said, " we are from America." "Well," they replied, "we don't consider you foreigners —only those from the continent." So we were photographed with our English cousins. I met with the three gentlemen who were to have met me at Exeter Hall the night previous. "You gave me a bitter experience by not coming back to the hall," I said. They all expressed themselves as being very sorry, and gave as the reason for not coming the lateness of the hour and the fearful storm. The closing exercises were held under the eaves of the castle. The Queen was at Balmoral,

Scotland; but as we gathered there I saw the maids with their fancy headgear, peeping from the windows. The singing was inspiring. Prayer was offered by the Rev. Mr. Krumacher, a celebrated German divine, and also by Dr. Cuyler, who afterwards gave a very eloquent address. Among the grand things he said was, "The memory of this meeting would warm the coldest night that Norway would ever know, and its influence would belt the entire globe." John Wanamaker also gave a fine address. One remark he made was this: "I shall never be able to find that word foreigner in my dictionary again." I turned to Mr. A—— and said: "I rubbed that out a long time ago." I think everyone felt that there were no lines drawn between us. And especially so when that vast multitude lifted up their voices, and sang the grand old doxology. I think as each of us slowly wended our way to the railway station, and took the train back to London, we felt that that meeting had been one of great profit, and we would all go back to our various fields of labor with a stronger purpose to work more earnestly for the Saviour of mankind. Mr. A—— secured lodging for me in the same house at which he was stopping. It was located on Montague street, a pleasant part of the city.

FRIDAY, June 8.—I concluded the best way to see the great city of London was on the top of an omnibus. So after I went to Upper Bedford street, Russell Square, to see about a permanent lodging place, I climbed to the lofty peak of an omnibus on Long Acre street, and was delighted with the part of the city we passed through. I went to the end of the route, then I went into the Victoria station. It seemed to be the starting point of a number of lines of coaches. I had a letter of introduction to a family at Stamford Hill, one of the suburbs of London. I inquired of one of the drivers if any of them ran in that direction. He pointed out one that did. I took a seat near the driver, who seemed delighted to answer the many questions I asked him as we drove through the busy streets for more than an hour before reaching our destination. He directed me how to reach Fairholt road, where this family lived. It was a walk of about six blocks. On either side of the street were neat little houses with yards in front, some of them tastefully arranged. On reaching the house I noticed on the gate the name of Hope Lodge. Most of the beautiful cottages in that locality had suggestive names. The door-bell was answered by a very neat, trim young lady (they styled her the maid of the house). I gave her my letter. She seemed to know something of my coming, for she at once invited me in, and showed me into the nicely furnished parlor, and went to call the lady, a Mrs. S——, a sister of an old friend of mine, Rev. C—— B——, in Camden, N. J. Presently a very fine, intelligent lady came in and said: "This is Mr. Butler; we have been looking for you for more than a week." Then the family, consisting of husband and three sons, were called in to see the lad fresh from America. I was not long in their presence before I found I was in a refined Christian home. I felt like adding to this "Hope Lodge" the other two names that mean so much, namely, Faith and Charity. The questions were many that were asked about the dear ones in America, whom they had not seen for many long years. They insisted on my remaining with them over night. I finally consented to do so. A gentleman and his wife living near came in and spent the evening. He was formerly from Edinburgh, Scotland, and entertained us with a discription of that country. After I listened to Mr. S—— describe London, I concluded it would take more time to see this interesting city than I had expected it would. He informed me that it had a population of over five millions, and began to enumerate the most prominent places of interest, until I almost concluded I would have to postpone sleeping and keep on the move continually in order to get through in the time I had planned to remain.

SATURDAY, June 9.—Mr. S—— and I started out shortly after breakfast, he having a little time to spend with me before going to business. The first place we visited was Abeney Park Cemetery, where quite a number of noted persons are sleeping. He took me to a beautiful spot in the cemetery, which was the favorite resort of Dr. Isaac Watts, where he wrote most of his hymns that have been blessing the world for years. I also saw his monument. I copied the following from it: "Erected as a testimony of the high esteem of his Christian character and valuable writing." I also saw the tomb of Henry Richards, the great "Peace Man," as he was called. Then I stood at the grave of Catherine Booth, the mother of the Salvation Army. On the tombstone were these words: "More than conquer through Him that hath loved us." And at the base these striking words: "Do you follow Christ?" After leaving this beautiful cemetery we rode down to City Road Chapel, a spot dear to every Methodist. This old chapel was built by the earnest efforts of the sainted John Wesley, and from this, the first Methodist church ever built has gone out, an influence that has touched the entire world, until to-day men everywhere are compelled to say the Methodist Church is a great power for good. I can never describe the feeling that took possession of me as I entered that historical edifice, and especially so when I stood in the old-fashioned pulpit where this man of God so often proclaimed the gospel, and then stood at the altar where he administered the sacrament of the Lord's Supper to those who are now with him in the Kingdom. I also sat in his quaint old chair. The design of the moulding around the gallery is a serpent coiling around a dove. Mr. Wesley's idea was: "As wise as serpents, and as harmless as doves." I sat in Mr. Fletcher's chair, and saw the font from his church at Madely. The janitor showed us through the vestry. There were an old table used by Mr. Wesley, and a clock that told the time to those who more than a hundred years have been in eternity. I held one of the old pewter collection plates that was used at the foundry where Wesley held his first service. I also sat on a bench used there. I saw a window frame that came from his old home. I copied from a silver plate taken from his coffin the words: "Johannes Wesley, Obin Do Du Marth, 1791." I saw Mrs. Charles Wesley's hymn book, also a book containing six hymns, in Charles Wesley's own handwriting. I said: "Thank God for inspiring this man to write so many sweet songs—especially the one sung the world over: 'Jesus, lover of my soul.'" The church, within a few years past, has undergone repairs.

The new columns are of jasper, given by the Methodist churches of America, North and South Australia, Canada and Ireland. We went out in the churchyard and stood by the grave of John Wesley. The tomb of the great Dr. Adam Clark is close beside it. The house in which Wesley died is near the chapel. We also visited Bunhill Cemetery, which is on the opposite side of the street. The dust of John Bunyan sleeps there. I also stood by the grave of Daniel De Foe, author of the famous book, "Robinson Crusoe," that I read with so much interest when a boy. He was born in 1661, and died in 1731. I then went to St. Giles' Church, at Cripple Gate. I saw the monument of the illustrious John Milton, and stood near the spot where he is buried. I copied from the marble slab on the floor the date of his birth and death : "Born, 1608; died, 1674." Oliver Cromwell was married in this old church. I copied from a tablet the name of Edward Harrison ; he died 1666. The monument of Rev. John Fox, author of "Book of Martyrs," is here also; he was once pastor of the church. From there I went to St. Bartholomew's, The Great. Mr. S—— informed me it was the oldest church in London; built in the eleventh century. I was wonderfully impressed as I walked over those old marble slabs, many of them worn down so that it was almost impossible to read the name on them. The old columns were eaten by the tooth of time. I copied from a tablet the name of F. Antoni, died 1641; also P. Sydenham, died 1593. The date on the altar was 1589. We then went to the great meat market. It is said to be the largest in the world. Some of the animals I saw hanging there once roamed the praires of America. In passing Great Queen Street Wesleyan Chapel I inquired of the janitor if he could direct me to a family where I could get a good lodging-room, for I failed to get one at Bedford Place. He sent me to one of their members, on Southampton row. She could not accommodate me, and directed me to a Mrs. C——, on Bernard street, Russell Square. I secured a room there, and it proved to be a very home-like place. The lady was a fine Christian woman, with four interesting children. A gentleman, a native of Calcutta, was rooming there. He was highly educated, and spoke English very fluently; he was one of the most polite men that I ever met. He was a Brahmin, and wrote out their order of worship for me, and also translated my hymn, "A Sinner Like Me," into their language.

Sunday, June 10.—I had an engagement with Mr. A——, the delegate from Dayton, Ohio, to go with him to Spurgeon's Tabernacle. We met at the Waterloo bridge, and walked to the Tabernacle, which is situated near the Elephant and Castle. I was reminded of the fact that a few nights previous I was wandering out in that direction searching for a refuge from the storm. The streets were thronged with people making their way to this wonderful place of worship. One might have thought the vast majority of people living in that vicinity were of the Baptist persuasion. It is an immense building, with a seating capacity of 6,000; it has three galleries. We were given seats near the pulpit, where we had a good view of that vast congregation. The precentor stood on the platform near the desk and led that multitude of people in songs that seemed to be familiar, for it appeared to me that from below where I sat, to the uppermost seat in the third gallery, everyone joined in those hymns of praise which were so inspiring. I felt as though heaven and earth were in touch with each other. The Rev. Mr. Spurgeon, son of the late beloved and widely known Rev. C. H. Spurgeon, preached from Psalms xli, 1. It was on the subject of Christian giving. It was a plain, practical sermon. I had heard him when he was visiting America a few years previous, at Bethany Presbyterian Church, Philadelphia. At the close of the service I felt amply paid for my long walk from Russell Square. Mr. A—— had another engagement, so I took a walk down to Westminster Abbey. I stood on the Westminster bridge and enjoyed the view of the fine buildings on each side of the Thames. The House of Parliament, a large, massive stone building, stands on the bank, looking as though it meant to remain there for centuries to come. I took a seat near the Abbey and engaged in conversation with a gentleman formerly from Birmingham. He informed me that the afternoon service at the Abbey commenced at 3 o'clock, so I concluded to remain in that locality and attend service at the place of worship that I had read and heard so much about. I shall not attempt to describe this great edifice now, but will give an outline of it later on. I went into the service and found a large congregation assembled. It was the day set apart once a year by all denominations throughout the city for taking collections for the various hospitals. The service was sung by one of the finest choirs I ever heard, after which the Dean of Gloucester preached a very able sermon from John xi, 3. If each one that listened to that sermon put it into practice, I am sure some of the poor of London were benefited. On my way from Westminster, just as I reached Trafalgar Square, where stands the monument of Nelson (a man whose memory is precious to every son and daughter of Old England), I saw the parade of the striking cabmen passing. The bands were playing lively airs, and the streets had the appearance of a gala day instead of the Sabbath. There were several hundred men in line. On their banners were inscriptions of various kinds, giving the spectators some idea of their grievances. They were on their way to Hyde Park to ventilate themselves on the question of right, from their standpoint. I found my way through the winding streets without much difficulty, reaching home in time for tea. In the evening I went to the Great Queen Street Wesleyan Chapel. It was built in 1817. It has two side galleries. The old-fashioned high pulpit stands in front of the chancel, and is nearly on a level with the first gallery. At one time it had a very large membership, but now it is comparatively small, owing to the fact of many of its members moving to different parts of the city. At the close of the service I met with a young man, one of the prominent members of the church, who invited me to take a walk with him. We walked a long distance. He pointed out many places of interest. One was Buckingham Palace, the Queen's London home. It is a massive building, with elegant grounds. I also saw the Prince of Wales' home. I concluded the royal family were well cared

for. The young man gave me his name as W——
S——, formerly from Yorkshire, and said he was a
salesman in a wholesale notion store at Cheapside. So
passed my first Sabbath in the wonderful city of
London.

MONDAY, June 11.—London seems to be built
something in the style of patchwork. I lived in
Russell Square. A few minutes' walk brought one to
Bloomsbury Square. Adjoining that was Montague
Square, which is a beautiful part of the city. Near by
is Lincoln-on-Field, and Holborn, and a number of
other districts. The old city of London has only about
100,000 inhabitants, and the police wear a little different
uniform. All these districts have been pieced on to
it until it has become the greatest city in the civilized
world. I had to meet Dr. R—— and Mr. A. M——
and wife, coming from Nottingham, at the St. Pancreas Station in the afternoon. So I spent part of the
morning in sightseeing from the top of the street-cars.
I rode to Islington, and was quite taken with the fine
array of stores. Then I found I had some time on my
hands before the arrival of the train, so seated myself
on the tram for a ride to the part of the city called
Mother Shipton. I was very curious to see what kind
of a place it was, with such an odd name, but found it
similar to some other parts I had visited. I was glad
to see some part of the ship's company, and felt as
though I was meeting friends of yore when Dr. R——
and Mr. A—— M—— and wife stepped from the train.
Doctor secured a room at the same place I was lodging. Then we took a stroll down the Strand, as far as
Charing Cross. The Strand is quite a thoroughfare.

There are some very attractive stores on it, and it is generally crowded with pedestrians and vehicles of all kinds. I saw a blockade on the Waterloo bridge which extended to the Strand. It was interesting to watch the police untangle it. Just by the raising of their hand the whole line would either move or stop, as they signaled. The Strand presents a gay appearance in the evening, as there are a number of places of amusement on this street and vicinity. The old Drury Lane Theatre, where the celebrated actress, Bell Gwynne, in the long-ago, drew the pleasure-seekers by the hundreds, is a short distance away.

TUESDAY, June 12.—We visited St. George's Catholic Cathedral, at the corner of Lambreth and St. George's road. The paintings were very attractive. We remained a short time at service. We also visited the great National Art Gallery, which is near the beautiful Trafalgar Square. The different schools of art are divided off into sections. In the Old British School there was a fine painting, entitled, "The Three Graces Decorating a Terminal Figure of Hymen," by Joshua Reynolds, in 1792; another, "The Watering Place," attracted my attention; "The Parson's Daughter," by George Romney, 1802, was beautiful. The artist must have found the sweetest face in all the kingdom to paint from. It was one that seemed to photograph itself on one's memory. In the French School was a landscape which was simply grand; also, "David at the Cave of Adullam," by Gelee; landscape, "Abraham and Isaac;" "A Seaport at Sunset," by Gelee. This was such a striking picture that I almost lost sight of the fact that there were hundreds of others to be seen. "The Embarkation of the Queen of Sheba," by Gelee, was a large, finely executed painting. In the Italian School there were: "A View of the Grand Canal, Venice," by Canale, 1768; "Christ and His Disciples at Emmaus," and "The Youthful Christ Embracing St. John." I lingered awhile, gazing at these two last mentioned paintings with thoughts that soared heavenward. A painting of an old woman peeling a pear was quite lifelike; "A Winter Scene in Germany," "The Triumph of Julius Cæsar," "Christ's Agony in the Garden"—a small picture, but very fine—by Allegrio, in the year 1234. In the School of Venice was the "Adoration of the Shepherds." This I thought magnificent. "The Baptism of Christ," by Embrian, 1492, was rather an odd painting. I also noticed "Music" and "Art," both famous paintings, about five feet high and three feet wide, done in high colors; two large, handsome paintings by Michael Angelo; one of them, "Christ on the Cross," and the other, "Christ being placed in the Tomb," attracted my attention. There was also a small, peculiar-looking picture, entitled, the "Virgin Enthroned," painted in the 15th century. I only made a note of one in the Spanish Department: Christ standing at the column, tied with a heavy rope, with a woman and child near by. I left the gallery, regretting I could not spend more time there. We made a very hurried visit to Guild Hall, where there are a number of fine paintings and pieces of statuary. Among them were a beautiul statue of Wellesly, Duke of Wellington, born 1769, died 1852; a large painting of the present Lord Mayor of London, at Windsor

Castle; a painting of the reception of King George III., April 23, 1789.

WEDNESDAY, June 14.—Went to hear the celebrated Dr. Parker, at his large temple at Holborn Viaduct. They have service every Wednesday. The temple was densely packed. I could only get a seat near the door. Dr. Parker is a fine, robust-looking man, and has a strong, commanding voice, so that I heard the discourse very distinctly. His subject was "Reconciliation." It was an able sermon, and was listened to with rapt attention by that vast audience. A lady sang a very affecting solo, entitled: "Bye and Bye." I had a letter of introduction to Mr. A——, brother of a friend of mine at Palmyra, N.J. He was an accountant on Gresham street, Cheapside. His partner, who was a member of the House of Commons, kindly gave me a pass for the Doctor and myself to visit the House during the session, so in the afternoon we went to the great House of Parliament. I had my overcoat on my arm (my overcoat and umbrella were my constant companions). The tall policeman that stood guard at the stairway evidently took me for a dynamiter, for he inquired very particularly what I had in my top coat pockets. I had two of my singing books, and made him feel easy by informing him it was nothing that would harm anyone. We were directed to the visitors' gallery and had a good view of some of the statesmen of Old England. The Speaker of the House sat in a large chair, with his wig and long coat on, looking quite ancient. There were several bills brought before the house, and debated on as earnestly as I had heard our American statesmen ventilate themselves on some great questions at the Capitol, at Washington, a few years ago. A representative of Old Ireland caused a roar of laughter by his clean-cut wit. The question they were talking on I did not get very clearly, but it was something in reference to a danger signal being placed on the rear of a train on a certain railroad. He quickly sprang to his feet and said in his rich brogue: "What is the use of that? I see no necessity for it, when they only have one train on that road." He excited their risibilities several times, but I was unable to catch the sharp things he was passing out. I am sure I shall always be grateful to Mr. C—— for his kindness in giving me the pass, for I considered it a great treat.

THURSDAY, June 14.—I visited the Westminster Abbey again. History tells us the present edifice, which is a grand structure, was built more than 600 years ago. The monastery was much older. It can be traced back from 900 to 1100 years, and when first established it stood on an island called Thorney, or Thorn Island, between the river Thames and the marshes which now form the water of St. James' Park. The monks here at first numbered only about twelve, but Edward the Confessor, who had his palace close by where now stands the House of Parliament, in the year 1065 enlarged it and made provision for about seventy monks. He erected a building for them, part of which is still standing. The old Abbey Church of Westminster was the first church in England built in the Norman style. When I entered this wonderful edifice a feeling of awe crept over me. It seemed like a huge sepulchre. Those spacious walls were covered with tablets; in every nook and corner stood the monuments and statuary of England's honored dead, as well as some from other countries. As I walked over those time-worn stone floors, I was busy with my pencil copying the names and epitaphs. I would like to be able to devote space enough to spread them out before my reader. I visited the tombs of the kings and queens. In St. Edwards' Chapel was the tomb of Edward the Confessor, who died January 5, 1066; Queen Editha, wife of Edward, died 1075; Queen Maud, died 1118; Edward I., died 1307. I wandered around where sleeps the royal dust of centuries until I almost forgot I was living in the nineteenth century. I was much interested in the poets' corner. I noticed the bust of Longfellow, our beloved American poet. It was placed there by his English admirers. There was a beautiful bouquet of fresh cut flowers at the base that some one had placed there that morning. I was intensely interested in the monument of Lady Nightingale, who died in 1734; it was of white marble. Death is represented as starting from beneath the monument and aiming his dart at Lady Elizabeth, who shrinks back into her husband's arms. It is said that a robber, who broke into the Abbey one night, was so terrified by Death's figure in the moonlight that he dropped his tools and fled in dismay. The epitaph of Sir John Franklin, the Arctic explorer, who lost his life, with all his crew, in 1847, when completing the Northwest passage, struck me as very good. It was by Tennyson. It reads as follows:

> " Not here : the white North has thy bones ;
> And thou, heroic sailor soul,

Art passing on thy happier voyage now,
Toward no earthly pole."

The coronation chairs claimed my attention for some time. One, it is said, was made for William's and Mary's coronation; the other for Edward I., to enclose the famous stone of Scone. Tradition identifies this stone with the one that Jacob rested his head upon at Bethel. Whether that be true or not, it has quite a history connected with it. When I left that historic old building I was reminded of a remark I heard a colored minister make in his sermon a few years ago, namely, "That death is a great leveler." I went to Cheapside, a noted business portion of the city. I made a hurried visit through the Old Bow Church, which is situated there. It is said that all who are born within the sound of the bells of this old church are called "Cockneys." From there I walked through the crowded streets to London Bridge. I asked a friend of mine, thoroughly acquainted with the city, where that wonderful tide of humanity came from that were going to and fro over this great bridge. He informed me that, independent of the city traffic, which is immense, there were hundreds of trains coming into the city, and there were a number of stations in the vicinity of the bridge, and the people from the trains greatly swell the number. It is estimated that 100,000 pedestrians and 20,000 vehicles cross this bridge daily. We went down to St. James' Park, and witnessed a fine drill of some of Old England's soldiers. I watched them with a great deal of interest. They presented quite a fine appearance. Some of them wore white coats, others red. They were accompanied by the

Grenadier Band, which went through almost as thorough a drill as the soldiers. They number seventy-five pieces, and discoursed some fine music. They gave a solo that amply paid me for the long journey there. We then joined the crowd that followed them to the Royal Palace grounds, and saw them drill, and also saw the Horse Guards go through a very fine drill. Mrs. M———'s father went with us, to see the American consul, to get a pass for us to visit Woolwich Arsenal, but he was not in, so we took a walk through that section of the city, which contains a great many handsome residences, and came up Regent and Oxford streets. There are a great many large and attractive stores on these two streets. It is a beautiful sight to see these streets illuminated, and I quite enjoyed a stroll through them.

FRIDAY, June 15.—Mr. and Mrs. M——— went with Dr. R——— and myself to the wonderful Zoological Garden. It is beautifully laid out, and contains a large collection of animals and birds from all parts of the world. We spent several hours there, and I have jotted it down as one of the principal places of interest in London. We came through the section of the city called Rotten Row. It is a very aristocratic locality, but one would not think so by the name. We also visited the British Museum. There is so much to be seen in this great museum that one needs plenty of time to see all of interest. I was so wonderfully interested that my friends grew weary of waiting for me while I inspected the relics of past ages. I was interested in a letter written by Queen Victoria, when a little girl; also signatures of the different kings and queens and prominent men of the past. I purposed coming again and spending more time there. I took a walk down the Strand, and on my way took the wrong street, and found myself in a rough locality. Some of the residents had been out making friendly calls and had tipped the bottle and had gotten greatly tangled up. I hurried out to the Strand as soon as possible. I concluded I was in a neighborhood where there might be a demand for my pocketbook.

SATURDAY, June 16.—Doctor R—— and I rode down to St. Martins street; from there to Westminster Bridge. There we took one of the little steamers up the Thames, to Chelsea, and were transferred to another steamer running to the noted Kew Gardens. It was a delightful day and the ride up the river was charming. We passed some fine residences. I quite admired the meadow land that gave the river a very picturesque border. We went through the Gardens; they cover an area of several hundred acres, and are laid out in beautiful walks, and contain shrubbery of all kinds, and choice plants and flowers. It reminded me of some parts of Fairmount Park. From there we walked up to Richmond, a short distance away. It is a beautiful town, of considerable size. There were very many houses that had the appearance of being very ancient, but most of the modern residences were similar to those in this section of our country. The young prince who made his advent into this old world during my sojourn in the United Kingdom, was born at White Lodge, Richmond. We then rode on the top of a tram to Kew, and went back to

Chelsea on the steamer; we stopped off there and walked through some part of the town. I jotted it down as another of London's beautiful suburban towns. We then seated ourselves on the top of an omnibus running direct to London Bridge. It was a long ride, but an enjoyable one. We passed through Piccadilly, Trafalgar Square, Charing Cross, the Strand, Cheapside, and Ludgate Circus. We left the coach at the monument and joined the multitude going to and fro over London Bridge. There is generally some excitement on this wonderful thoroughfare. We had not proceeded far on the bridge before we discovered a crowd gathered around some object of interest. My curiosity led me to investigate it. I found it to be a young man kindly caring for a very respectable looking young girl, who seemed to be suffering from general debility, caused by lifting the "little brown jug" too often. We say, "God save our young men from intemperance." My observation leads me to say, "God save our young women, who are in great danger also." A little further on we noticed another group of men and boys; a poor old horse had suddenly laid down the burden of life, and they were viewing his remains. After going over near where I spent my first night in the city, we returned and went to the district of Whitechapel. Whitechapel road is quite a broad thoroughfare, many of the houses quite large, but the lanes and alleys leading into it are filled with men and women far down in the scale of morality. We met a great number of these wretched characters marketing. I thought, as I looked at them, this is the result of letting the devil take the helm; he is sure to run us on the rocks of sin and wreck us if he has the guiding of our craft. I was not surprised at the wholesale murders that have been committed there. In the evening we took a walk through Red Lion street, West Centre, a long, narrow street, containing a variety of little shops on either side. It was rather difficult elbowing our way through the crowded thoroughfare. Some of the stores looked as though they were built when London was a little village.

SUNDAY, June 17.—I had an engagement with Mr. W—— to meet him at the Bow Church, at Cheapside, and go with him to St. James' Hall, Piccadilly, but I was detained and missed him. I walked down to St. Paul's Cathedral, and stepped in to service. The singing, like that at Westminster Abbey, was excellent. There was assembled a large, attentive congregation. The seats were old-fashioned. Many of them were old rush-bottomed chairs. All the cathedrals I visited were furnished in like manner, and all of them had stone floors. I remained only a short time, then took a long walk to St. James' Hall. I reached there in time to hear Rev. Mark Guy Pearce preach a very excellent sermon from the text, " If God So Clothed the Grass of the Fields," etc. He illustrated his simple, comprehensive sermon by a blade of grass, which he held up before that immense congregation, and I think every one was impressed, after listening to him, with God's great care over us. I stood on the corner of a street conversing with one of the members of his congregation, and as this famous preacher and his wife were about to pass us, this gentleman called to them and I was introduced, and walked with them nearly to Russell Square. I found Mr.

Pearce a very genial and interesting man. In the afternoon I went to the Great Queen Street Mission School, on Princess street, a small thoroughfare running off Red Lion street. I was called upon to make an address. Many of the children were the offspring of poor, degraded people. The little ones listened very attentively as I told them of our schools over in the great country of America. I met Mr. H—— S——, a member of a large Bible class at the church. He insisted that I should take tea with him, and I finally consented to do so. I found his family of the good old English type. They live at the Freemason's Hall, his father having charge of it. I was shown through that beautiful hall. I saw the handsome chair that the Prince of Wales occupies when he attends the lodge. There was a collection of regalias, and paraphernalia, and curiosities of different kinds, which I was interested in. I always found the " latch-string " out for me at that home, and regard them as among the number of friends I left when I sailed from the shores of Old England. In the evening I again went to St. James' Hall and heard Rev. Hugh Price Hughes, who also is a noted minister of the gospel. Rev. M. G. Pearce and he are co-laborers in mission work at Piccadilly. I was surprised to meet the young man there with whom I had the conversation at Westminster.

MONDAY, June 18.—I visited the British Museum. It was only a short distance from my lodging place. I was there as soon as it was open for visitors. It would take too much space to give a very elaborate discription of this interesting place. One could spend days there looking at relics of the past ages, and curiosities from all parts of the world. I will only give a few which I have jotted down. I saw some stones from the great temple of Ephesus, A.D. 104, inscribed with public documents relating to a bequest of Salutans to the town of Ephesus; also stones from the temple of Diana, at Ephesus, inscribed with a decree conferring citizenship and other honors, B.C. 300; wall stones of Temple Preene, B.C. 240; bust of Periander, about B.C. 600, from Villa Montalts, Rome; a bust of Demosthenes, born B.C. 383, died B.C. 323; bust of Metrodorus, who flourished about B.C. 460; a Greek inscription from Thessalonica; a stone with inscriptions, from Athens, B.C. 415; carved figures from India, representing persons in a devotional attitude. A clock made by Isaac Habsect, of Strasburg, 1589, of brass, stood on a wooden base. It has figures of ladies carved on brass plates, the lower one balancing scales in her hands. It is a wonderful piece of mechanism. Also, a large enameled plate with the figure of Christ on the cross; from Herring Islands, a trap for catching a kind of fish called soles; it was a rope with a curious looking loop. In the Fiji Island department, I saw human bones from a cannibal feast; they were fixed in the stump of a tree. A curious musical instrument, from the river Niger; it was in the shape of a boat; also a war trumpet about five feet long. I saw mummies that are said, by good authority, to be wives of the three Pharaohs. I was so intensely interested that I neglected to look after the inner man, until about 4 P. M. I was looking at a very ancient piece of music. I called the attention of a young man standing near me to it. In conversation with him, he informed me he was from Philadelphia, and gave his name as Dr. K——, connected with one of the hospitals there. After dining together, we parted with a promise to meet at Trafalgar Square on Saturday. I was greatly amused at seeing a woman driving a small donkey to a miniature cart loaded with cabbage; she sat on top of the choice vegetables, guiding the animal skilfully through the crowded street. It looked like a sewer rat harnessed up.

TUESDAY, June 19.—I took a ride to Peckham to call on the brother of Mr. H——, of Camden, N. J. On my way down Walworth road, I saw a small street called East street. It was crowded with people. I thought I would see what the attraction was. I found it was a curbstone market. They were selling articles of every conceivable sort. I was amused at them selling fish; the proprietor of the stand would cut off a piece and auction it off by the pennyworth. In the evening I took a long ride to the home of Mrs. M——'s father, on Ezra street, off Columbia road. The old gentleman seemed delighted in showing me around that vicinity, which is a fine locality. There is a large museum near by.

WEDNESDAY, June 20.—Mr. M—— and wife, Dr. R—— and I took a steamer at London Bridge for Greenwich. I had a grand view of the shipping of London as we passed down the river. Greenwich is a very old town, and is packed full of interest. I would have liked to have spent the day there. We took the train for Woolwich, to visit the arsenal. As I passed through the barracks, I was amused at some of the raw recruits trying to mount their horses in military style. We went to the Rotunda, where they have a number of old guns stored. One old gun was made in 1525, another in 1751. A very handsome one was made for Napoleon in the 17th century. I noticed an old lock made in 1666, an old rifle made in 1672, an English breech-loader made in 1600. I also saw a brass cannon, presented to Her Majesty, Queen Victoria, by Napoleon III., 1858; also the original armor of a knight of St. John, 1260; fowling gun of James II., 1683; one belonging to William III., 1506. The janitor showed us a gun made in 1744, in which glass balls were used; they were aimed at the enemy's eyes. There was a gun inlaid with ivory; it was a fine piece of work. I saw the gun that sunk the "Mary Rose," 1583, afterward raised in 1836. We then went through every department of the arsenal, where all the firearms are made, which is well worth a visit. We saw them making some immense cannon. When busy they employ 17,000 men. We were informed that there were about 15,000 at work there. It was a sight when they came out of the yard at twelve o'clock for dinner. We took the train for Cannon street, reaching home at 7 P. M.

THURSDAY, June 21.—Went to Hyde Park, one of the finest I have ever seen. It is finely laid out. The drives are beautiful. I saw a great many very handsome teams. I was convinced, as I saw the people driving in such elegant style, that London had a great number of wealthy families. We walked through the Park to the Albert Memorial; it is near the Albert Memorial Hall; it was erected to the memory of the late Prince Consort; it consists of a bronzed gilt statue of the Prince Consort under a Gothic canopy, and surmounted by four groups of statuary. We then went to South Kensington Museum. There is a fine collection of relics and curiosities there. The building is very large. I saw the model of the warship Caledonia, launched at Plymouth 1809 ; a model of the Eddystone Light, 1757–1759. I was interested in the State Barge built in the reign of King James I. ; it carried 21 oars, and was 63 feet in length ; the cabin was decorated with heavy gilt moulding and finished in red oak, with red and gilt furniture ; the stern was handsomely carved and heavily gilded. It had been used as a pleasure boat for the royal family. I saw an imitation in wood of a Rhine salmon caught in the Rhine January 4, 1868; it weighed 51½ pounds. Also a gondola used at Venice. I was interested in the works of a large clock made by Peter Lightfoot, one of the resident monks of Gladstonbury Abbey, 1325. In the reign of Queen Elizabeth it was removed to Wells' Cathedral, where it was used until about fifty years ago. I copied from a tablet under the clock the following : "This claims attention, it being the work of one man, and its association with Gladstonbury ; it indicates the day and night, and age of the moon ; framing and wheels wrought in iron and fastened together with mortar and terra cotta." There were also two historic bells from Gladstonbury and Wells' Cathedral. We paid a hurried visit to the Imperial Institute ; it is a very imposing building. The interior is beautiful. In the evening, coming from Stamford Hill, we discovered a large fire. It appeared to me that all that part of London was on the move in the direction of it. When we reached a certain point we left the car, which was blocked, and moved slowly with the crowd. It was a large furniture place not far from old City Road Chapel that was burning. They considered the Chapel in great danger at one time. It was nearly 12 o'clock when we reached home.

FRIDAY, June 22.—I spent most of the day at my favorite place, the British Museum. There are so many relics there from the towns mentioned in the Bible. I purchased a guide book and marked the principal objects of interest, instead of using my note book. Unfortunately I left it on the other side of Old Ocean, If the reader contemplates a trip to London, he should not fail to spend several days at the British Museum. In the afternoon I took the train at Victoria Station for Suydenham, where the wonderful crystal palace is situated. I found it was rather late to see very much of the palace, so concluded to postpone my visit to it, and take a stroll through the town. I found it quite a beautiful place; the "shops" were quite attractive, especially on the main street, near the palace. On the streets surrounding this great crystal palace are elegant residences, with grounds tastefully laid out. I was informed that it would take me more than one day to see all the objects of interest in the palace, and judging from the large area of ground it covered, I was convinced it would. I went to a restaurant to take the edge off my appetite, and just as I entered the door I heard a startling scream. I found a lady greatly excited. Her daughter was in the act of pouring a bucket of hot tea into the reservoir, when she fell from the chair, receiving a shower-bath of scalding tea. We supposed at first it was very serious, but it proved to be otherwise. I managed to get some attention after the excitement subsided. On the arrival of the train at Victoria Station, I went to Great Queen Street Chapel. I began to feel quite at home there.

SATURDAY, June 23.—Dr. R—— and I were to to meet Dr. K—— at Trafalgar Square, and go with him to several places of interest. The House of Parliament is open on Saturday to the public. We went first through the House of Lords, a magnificent part of the building. It was richly furnished, and the carving on the mouldings was one of the finest pieces of work I have ever seen. I greatly admired the beauty of the Queen's robing-room. Then I went through the House of Commons again. The gentlemen who were airing themselves on various questions of the day, when I was there before, had all "dispersed and wandered far away." They hold no session on Saturdays. There are a number of fine pieces of statuary of some of England's honored statemen, placed about in different parts of the House; the greater part, however, are in the main hallway. We then went to the old St. Margaret's Church. It is beside the Westminster. This is a very historic church. The Cavendish memorial window is beautiful; in it different parts of the Bible are represented in bright colors. "My flesh shall rest in hope," this is illustrated by the taking of Christ from the cross. "Peace be still," by Jesus appearing to His disciples on the sea. It was a masterpiece of work, and greatly to be admired. We sat in the pew set apart for Americans. It had the American flag inserted in each arm of the seat, with these words: "For visitors from the United

States." The janitor told us that General Grant sat in that seat when visiting London several years ago. The janitor invited us to remain to a wedding that was to take place. So we seated ourselves in the seat for Americans of *low* as well as of high degree; but just before the wedding party arrived we were informed that it was against the rules for us to remain—not being invited guests. The janitor said to us, as we were leaving: "There is to be a grand wedding here this afternoon, and I am to attend the door, and I will see that you get in, if you desire to." But so far as I was concerned, I had seen so many launch out on the "sea of matrimony" that I thought I could find something that would interest me more than that. We rode up to Chauncey lane. There Dr. R—— left us. We went to St. Paul's Cathedral. History tells us that this is the third cathedral built on this spot. The first one was built A.D. 607, and was destroyed by fire in 1087; it was rebuilt, and destroyed again by the great fire in 1662. After that it was rebuilt by Christopher Wren, the corner stone being laid in 1675. The building opened for divine service in 1697. The interior length is 502 feet, exclusive of projection of portico, from north to south, including the semicircular porticos, 244 feet. The western front is 177 feet; the diameter of drum beneath the dome is 112 feet; the dome itself is 102 feet; the height of the central aisle is 89 feet; the total height from the pavement of the churchyard to the top of the cross is 370 feet. I have given these dimensions as I found them in the "St. Paul's Guide." It is a wonderful structure. There are a great number of busts, statuary and tablets of prominent persons, who have passed away during the past centuries. On the altar, which is handsome, is a representation of Christ on the cross, with cherubs around Him. Near the altar rail is a monument of Reginald Heber, D.D., late Bishop of Calcutta, who died in 1826. The Vice Admiral Horatio Viscount Nelson, H.B., must have immortalized himself with the English nation, judging from the inscription which I copied; it was as follows: "To record his splendid and unparalleled achievements during a life spent in the service of his country, and terminated in the moment of victory, by a glorious death, in the memorable action off Cape Trafalgar, on October 21, 1805." He was born in 1758. There were tablets with records of officers and privates who died from wounds and diseases during the war with Russia, 1855–1856. There is a tablet to Major Charles George Gordon, "who at all times gave his strength and substance to the poor, his sympathy to the suffering, and his heart to God." The monument to William Viscount Melbourne, Prime Minister in the last four years of King William IV.'s reign, and the first four of Queen Victoria's, born 1779, died 1848, is an arch representing gates, with statues of two angels on each side; over the door are these words: "Through the gate of death we pass to our joyful resurrection." I saw the tombs of Nelson and Duke of Wellington. I also saw the funeral car of Wellington; it is said to be made of the different cannon captured in the many battles he was engaged in; it is a wonderful piece of work. From the crypt we went to the whispering dome. I could hear the attendant speaking distinctly, although some distance away. Out on the balcony, we had a grand view of the city. I had some idea of the immense space it occupied. Don't fail to visit old St. Paul when in London. From there we visited the Tower of London. I shall give only a brief description of it, although it is full of interest. The guide book informs us that it owes its origin to the Romans, so it dates far back into the past. In the crown-room are some costly old relics: Knight of Garter, a fine emblem given by the corporation; St. Edward's crown; crown of King James II.; the imperial state crown of Queen Victoria is a sceptre with cross studded with diamonds; the Prince of Wales' crown, neat and plain; the crown of the consort of King James II. is small, but handsome; a cross of diamonds. All the crowns and smaller relics are kept in a large glass case with an iron railing encircling it. Inside the railing was a desk belonging to King William and Mary; an elegant gold sacramental falcon; a handsome christening fount about three feet high and two feet wide. In another department I saw the block that Lord Lovat was beheaded on and the axe that was used; also instruments of torture such as thumb-screws, etc.; also an old saddle, embroidered with gold, belonging to the Duke of York; armor of Charles II. when a boy; an imitation of Prince of Wales' wedding cake; it was a huge affair. I stood on the spot where Queen Anne Boylen and Lady Jane Grey were executed. Afterward I went into the department once used as a prison where these two women, with a number of prominent persons far back in the past, were imprisoned. The old walls were covered with inscriptions. I purchased a book with some of the inscriptions in. I will give a few.

Some of the words are spelled in queer style, "Authur Pool, I. H. S. A passage perillus maketh^e a port pleasant, A.D., 1568;" "Charles Bailey, Be frend to one, be ennemy" to none, Anno. 1571-10 Sept. The most unhapy man is he that is not pacient in adversities for men are not killed with adversities, but with ye impacience which they suffer." Another, "Philip Howard Earl, of Arundel. It is a reproach to be bound in the cause of sin, but to sustain the bonds of prison for the sake of Christ is the greatest glory;" this was was written on the old wall, May 1587. The Tower is open on Saturdays for visitors, free of charge. From the tower we took a walk down along the Thames embankment to Waterloo bridge.

SUNDAY, June 24.—Walked over to City Road Chapel to the service. They use the ritual; it was much like the low Episcopal service, and was very impressive. The sermon was such that one could easily follow the thread of it. The choir was quite large and contained some fine voices. The organist is the grandson of the sainted Charles Wesley. I had the pleasure of shaking his hand at the close of the services. I spoke to him of the great influence that his grandfather and great uncle, John Wesley, exerted, their work for the Master being felt all over America. He pressed my hand warmly and replied: "I am glad of it." In the evening I went to Liverpool Road Wesleyan Church. After service at the church quite a number of the members assembled in a small street just off St. Pancreas Road and held services. They had a small organ and two of the young men had cornets, and when they all began to sing the crowd soon gathered about them. One man began to exhort the unsaved to come to the Saviour of all mankind. When the crowd grew restless, they charmed them with some sweet songs again. I was delighted with the service. After it closed several of the young men walked down home with me. I found them earnest Christians.

En=Route for Scotland.

MONDAY, June 25.—I arose early and began making preparations to leave the city where I had spent three weeks, the recollections of which will not soon be brushed from memory's wall. I went to the great Bank of England to get a note changed. It was well worth the long walk I took to get there. It is quite an institution. The gold coins piled up made one feel a little envious. I called to see my friend W——, at Cheapside. He said he had written to his father that I would break my journey at York and go to Brompton and remain with them over night, and he insisted on me doing so. With a great many regrets I left London at 5 P. M. Dr. R.—— left on the steamer for Edinburgh, Scotland. I passed through a number of fine towns, one of them being Bedford, where the noted John Bunyan wrote his widely-known book, "Pilgrim's Progress." Two ladies got in the car there and I engaged in conversation with them. They gave me a little history of the old town. I arrived at Birmingham at 8:30, rode out to Harborn, and received a very cordial welcome at my English home.

TUESDAY, June 26.—Left Birmingham for the old city of York; passed through the large cities of Derby, Chesterfield, and Sheffield, arriving at York at 3 P. M. This was one of the most interesting cities I visited.

History tells us that the Romans occupied this site for more than three centuries. The Emperor Severus is said to have died in York in 211, A.D., also Constantius, in 306, A.D. Henry II. held his first parliament here in 1160. March 1190, several hundred Jews sacrificed their lives to popular hatred. The first church was built for Christian worship in the year 627, and stood where the large and finely built Yorkminster now stands. This Cathedral was completed 1472. I was charmed with its beauty. Surely back in those days they had fine ideas of architectural beauty. The old walls still surround the city. It is said they were originally built by the Romans. I walked around them and had a good view of the city. As I walked through the old streets, and saw so many quaint looking buildings, I was so taken with it that I decided to spend another day there. I met an old lady on the street. She was distributing tracts. I stopped and had quite a long conversation with her. She gave me some valuable information in reference to the city. I understood from a gentleman that I afterward met, she was in that locality every day giving tracts to all the passersby. Sometimes persons treated her rudely, but if a soldier lad was passing at the time he would step in between her and the one illtreating her and say to him : "Don't you hurt that old gal." He said she had the profound respect of the soldiers. I saw a great number of the redcoats on the streets. Took the train for Brompton, some twenty miles away, arriving at 6:30, and found the family of my friend W—— looking for me. They gave me a welcome that I shall not soon forget. The family at home consisted of father, mother, two daughters and three sons. They were a very musical family, and I was quite charmed with their singing. The old gentleman was a fine basso singer, and both the young ladies played the piano finely. My autoharp quite interested them, as they had never seen one before. They kept me up singing and chatting until long after 12 o'clock.

WEDNESDAY, June 27.—I was quite surprised when Mrs. W—— informed me that she had never been to the city of York, only twenty miles away, notwithstanding she was born in that locality. I told them I was so delighted with the old city I intended to go back and spend another day there. They insisted on my returning and spending another night with them. One of the young men walked to North Allerton, a distance of two miles, with me. Like the town of Brompton, it is very old. It was market day and I quite enjoyed the sight of the market people with their produce spread out on the street and in the market house, that had stood the storms of long, long years. Went back to York, and while standing on the old bridge spanning the river Ouse, I inquired of a young man near me what old building that was near the bridge. He informed me it was Clifford's Tower, where, in the original tower, 2,000 Jews were massacred. He gained my confidence, and I walked with him around the old walls, passed through several old gates; he pointed out to me the King James' old palace, now used as a blind asylum, and I went through it. One of the little blind boys acted as guide. He took me through each department, and would stop for a few minutes to get his bearings and then proceed. I was very much interested in him as well as in the institution. I passed through an old street called the Shambles; the houses were very old, built so that each floor projected beyond the lower one, making their roofs nearly meet with those on the opposite side of the street. I found myself stopping and gazing about like a boy making his first visit to the city. I then went into the courtyard of King William's old palace, now used for the parish poor. I thought, what a change! Once the home of royalty, now the abode of the lowly. From there I went to Foss Gate, to the Merchant's Adventurer Hall. The lady having charge said, as she took me through: "The Merchants of York have been meeting here for 800 years, and it is still used as a business room." There is an old chapel connected with it that was built in 1411, and pewed in 1663. They were repairing it. I gathered up a wooden pin from one of the old rafters as a relic. She remarked: "Here is where the merchants attend service before going to sell their wares." I replied: "I think most of them the world over sell their wares, and, if they have time, then say their prayers." I left this charming old city regretting I could not spend more time there, and returned to Brompton and spent another evening with that fine old Yorkshire family, whom I shall always remember very kindly.

THURSDAY, June 28.—Left for North Allerton at 10:30; from there was booked, as they style it, for Edinburgh, Scotland. I broke my journey at Durham. The town is very ancient. The Cathedral, one of the largest and finest in England, stands on a very high hill overlooking the town. A beautiful river winds its way through a very picturesque valley. There is an old castle near the Cathedral which was built in 1093, by William, the Conqueror. There were a great many visitors, as there was a Sunday school excursion from a town on the borders of Scotland. I went through the Cathedral and then up in the dome, and had a grand view of the surrounding country, and was wonderfully pleased with the scenery. Left early in the afternoon for Newcastle-on-Tyne. It is a great ship-building town, but not much of interest to the sightseer is there. I rode on top of a tram through a fine part of the city. It was a general holiday, and everyone seemed bent on having a good time. There had been a race at the fair grounds, and as I was going to the station I met a great throng of people returning from it. I left for Edinburgh, glad to be on the move again. I was interested in the old walls at Berick, on the coast. A gentleman informed me that, centuries ago, a great many battles had been fought there. It is a large town in Scotland, just over the line. The scenery was fine. The cattle, grazing on the sides of the green hills, made a beautiful picture. I arrived in Edinburgh at 10 P. M. and found my way to the Y. M. C. A. hall, and learned the whereabouts of Dr. R———. A young man kindly took me to the hotel where the Doctor had secured a good room for me.

FRIDAY, June 29.—Edinburgh is divided by a broad valley of gardens. Princess street, one of the principal thoroughfares, is beautiful; it is terraced on the new side of the city, and contains some very large, attractive stores. On the opposite side of the valley is the famous Edinburgh Castle, perched on a rock 300 feet above the surrounding valley and 445 feet above sea level; the old part of the city slopes down from this rock. I have always heard that Edinburgh is one of the finest cities in the world, being referred to as the "Modern Athens. As I rode on the top of the tram along Princess street and looked down on those gardens, so tastefully arranged in the valley below, and then at the old castle, standing far above the city on that huge rock, I concluded that, of all the cities I had visited, its beauty could not be excelled. I went to the house that John Knox lived in from 1559–72, and in which he died. A quaint old inscription is on the outside of the house: "Lofe. God. above- al and your neichtbour as yi self." We went down through Cannon Gate, which is called the Whitechapel of Edinburgh. A great many little closes (or courts, as we would call them) lead from this street, whose entrances are quite narrow, but the enclosures a trifle wider, each containing several houses, wretched looking places, as are also many of the occupants. At that time the smallpox was quite prevalent in that section of the city, and I hesitated about taking the risk of going through. Dr. R—— said he thought there was no danger, but, as I saw the red flags hanging from the windows in all directions, I passed along rather hurriedly. A few minutes' walk brought us to Holyrood Palace and the Abbey, where the attendant informed us it would be opened for visitors an hour later. In looking up the history of this place, I learned that the Abbey was founded by King David I. The palace was begun by Charles IV., and burned by the English in 1544, and again by Cromwell's soldiers in 1650. Queen

Mary spent most of her time here. As we stood by the gate, the room that Rizzio was assassinated in while at supper with Mary was pointed out to us. The deed was done by Darnley, Ruthven and others in 1566. We was quite anxious to pay a visit to this historic place, but our time was limited. We went to the drill-ground at the base of the hill, which is 822 feet high, on the top of which is Arthur's famous Seat. A short distance away were the ruins of St. Anthony's Chapel. We stood and gazed very wistfully at the top of Calton Hill and Arthur's Seat, but knew it meant too much labor to reach the summit. We witnessed a fine military display. The cavalrymen handled their horses skilfully, showing excellent training; the Scottish Highlanders, with their plaid kilts, were quite attractive, and went through a very interesting drill. Several of them were detailed to go up the mountain—as I styled it—and when some distance away sounded their bugles, and a number of their comrades answered the call and ran up the side of the mountain as dexterously as goats. The band discoursed some fine old Scotch airs, that quite charmed me. We visited the Edinburgh Castle, which was considered a stronghold prior to the days of gunpowder, but which is now used as an infantry barracks for 1,200 men, and has an arsenal containing 30,000 stands of arms. We saw the State Prison, where the adherents of the Stuarts were confined, and passed through the old palace yard, then into the old crown-room, where are kept the regalias, or, as they are sometimes called, the honors of Scotland. The crown of Robert Bruce, with which Charles II. was crowned, is beautiful, as is also the sceptre. I was greatly interested in many other relics that I saw there. My notes were hurriedly taken as I passed through. Queen Mary's bed-room was a small apartment; in this room her son, James VI., was born. I had a good view of the country from the little window, from which it is said the infant Prince James was lowered in a basket to his mother's friends, to be educated in their faith. This portion of the castle was built by Queen Mary in 1565, and is on the edge of a rock 300 feet above the valley. I was quite interested in Queen Margaret's old church. It is on the highest part of the castle, and is the oldest building in Edinburgh, having been built in 1050. For many years it was used as a magazine, but, through the efforts of Dr. Daniel Wilson, it was restored in 1853. It is quite a small edifice, and contains a beautiful little window presented by Queen Victoria. I stopped at the barracks of the Scottish Guards, which certainly are comfortable quarters. I engaged in conversation with one of the soldiers, who said: " I have just returned from a visit home, and feel unfitted for duty. I shall not be able to settle down to this kind of life for several days. A fellow feels a ' wee bit ' bad in leaving the folks, especially mother." I became very much interested in this young man, and passed him out a huge bundle of sympathy, and gave him one of my hymn books and called his attention to the hymn, "A Sinner Like Me." He said: "I will read it, and keep it to remember you by." On the bomb battery stands Mons Meg, a very large gun, made at Mons, Belgium, 1476. From this battery I had a grand view of the city and surrounding country.

Edinburgh has a population of 345,000, suburbs included. We came down High street, once considered one of the finest streets in Europe, but time has robbed it of its beauty, and a great many of the old houses are crumbling with age. We visited Natural Art Gallery, which contains a number of fine paintings of celebrated artists. The statue of Burns is here. In the museum are a number of very old relics, among them being John Knox's pulpit, from St. Giles' Church. Scott's handsome monument stands near the Art Gallery. Under the canopy is a statue of Sir Walter Scott. It is quite an ornament to Princess street. Some distance away is the monument of Robert Burns—but these two men would live in the memories of lovers of their works without a marble shaft. We went by trim to Leith, and from there by steamer to the wonderful Firth Bridge. My guide book gives its dimensions as being 1½ miles long; the height of the cantilevers, 360 feet; length of central girders, 350 feet; length of large spans, 1,710 feet; headway above high water mark at centre of spans, 150 feet; the weight of iron and steel used, 54,000 tons. There were 500 accidents occurred during the seven years they were building it; 57 of them ending fatally. Our little steamer passed under the bridge and landed at South Queen's Ferry, a short distance below. We remained on the steamer and returned to Leith again. We took a trip to Portabella, a watering place a few miles from Edinbugh. It is quite a nice little seaside resort. They have small cars in which the bathers change their clothing. Horses are attached to the cars and they are taken out a certain distance and the bathers step from the cars into the surf. The ladies and gentlemen are not allowed to bathe together. One of the bathing masters told me they were not permitted to come within a certain distance of each other. I gave him a discription of an American seaside resort, where hundreds of men, women and children bathe together, and it is considered within the bounds of propriety.

SATURDAY, June 30.—Rode from Princess street through one of the finest parts of the city to the Botanical Gardens. As my time was limited, I could only hurriedly cast my eyes about, but saw enough to convince me that any admirer of plants and flowers could spend a day there nicely. On my return called on the secretary of the Y. M. C. A., and was much pleased with him; he spoke of their good work, but remarked that if the young men were more actively engaged in Christian work, they would not need so much else to interest them. They have a finely equipped hall. Dr. R—— left for Glasgow in the morning, and I left at 1:20 for Sterling, to visit the gentleman I met the first night I spent in London. We passed over the Forth bridge and through Alloa, a town of considerable size, having the appearance of being quite a business place. The country between Edinburgh and Sterling is very pretty. We arrived at 3 P. M., and I found my way to the home of Mr. J——. He and his good wife gave me a reception that assured me I was welcome. He had a trip arranged for himself and I, so after partaking of some refreshments, we went by train to Callender, which is a pleasant little town, then walked a distance of three miles along the Pass of Leny, to Loch Lubnaig, a beautiful sheet of water about 5 miles long and 1 mile broad. It is of considerable depth, but the water is so clear we could see the pebbles at the bottom. It abounds with fish; I saw a number of them exercising their fins. On the opposite side stands Ben Ledi, a grand old mountain, covered with verdure, lifting its head above the valley to the great height of 2,871 feet. The scenery was subline and I drank it in with a relish, and Mr. J——, who is a great lover of nature and of poetry also, informed me that he never tired of visiting that romantic spot. He also remarked that this was one of the places from which Sir Walter Scott received his inspirations when he wrote some of his beautiful poems. I am not surprised that lovers of poetry are charmed with his beautiful word-pictures taken from this beautiful spot. Near the Falls of Leny is the churchyard and chapel of St. Bride, spoken of in the "Lady of the Lake." I copied from the only remaining tombstone the name of P. McKinley, died 1825. We passed a number of the old thatched roofed cottages, some of them with huge rosebushes climbing up their sides. They had an air of neatness and comfort about them, and seemed quite homelike. I was reminded of the poem of Robert Burns, entitled "The Cotter's Saturday Night." When we were returning from Callender there was a very poor woman with two small children in the compartment with us. She had walked from her home in the highlands, a distance of sixteen miles, and begged money at Callender to pay her fare to the Bridge of Allen. She was going to the military camp at Cambusbarron, two miles from Sterling, to see her husband. My friend, Mr. J——, whose heart seemed to be as large as the world, interested himself in her, and gave her a ticket to complete her journey to Sterling, and then called the attention of all those in the compartment to her destitute condition. I was wonderfully pleased with the promptness with which each one responded. Some of them were men who were rough and profane, but had hearts full of sympathy. I quite admired those warm-hearted Scotchmen, and am sure, as the shillings and sixpences were passed to her, the look of gratitude which she gave to those who had shown her this kindness more than repaid them for the little sacrifice they had made.

SUNDAY, July 1.—Mr. J—— had arranged to go to Cambusbarron, a little village two miles from Sterling, to attend the joint meeting of the Young Men's and Young Women's Christian Association. It was quite an enjoyable walk over the hills. On reaching the hall we found a large audience assembled. I had only been seated a few minutes before they began singing my old hymn, "Saves a Poor Sinner Like Me." I can never describe my feelings as I listened to them singing it as heartily as I ever heard it sung in America. I thought, is it possible the piece which I wrote a number of years ago, and which I did not think would get beyond my own little city, has found its way over into the highlands of Scotland? I thanked God for inspiring me to write those words, which have been such a blessing to the world. I was called on to give them a short address, which I did, and at the close was invited by the superintendent of the Sunday school to address the convention, which met previous to the regular session. Mr. J——'s parents lived in the village, so I was taken through the quaint old streets to their cottage. The family at home consisted of father and mother, one daughter, (a young lady,) and two sons; one of them a young man, the other a lad of about fifteen years. The first thing this fine old Scotch lady did after I was introduced was to prepare some refreshments for me. I never visited that little cottage, no matter at what hour of the day, but the neat little tray was brought to me with something to tempt my appetite. Mr. J——'s father was an invalid, and had been for a number of years. He was a fine old Scotch character, and a man of considerable intelligence, and I quite enjoyed hearing him converse. The convention was held in the Presbyterian church. The congregation were principally the parents of the scholars, with a sprinkling of children. The pulpit was one of those high, old-fashioned ones, with winding steps. I said to my friend, "I think I shall beg to be excused from taking my position up there. I will be conspicuous enough down below." He replied, with a merry twinkle in his eye, "I think you will have to speak from the pulpit." Sure enough, the superintendent insisted upon my coming up with him. I should like to have a photograph of my tall form climbing the stairway and standing in the pulpit, with my head about even with the gallery. I felt rather awkward perched up there, and am sure it must have been rather trying on the necks of those who sat near the pulpit. I made the acquaintance of some very excellent people in the village, and will always remember my visits to their hospitable homes. In the evening, as we passed through the streets of Sterling, I saw quite a large number of people assembled in front of one of the Presbyterian churches, holding services, and was informed it was the custom of the members of this, as well as of other denominations, to hold their early services on the street, and that great good had been accomplished by them.

Monday, July 2.—Mr. J—— C—— and two of Mr. J——'s "wee bairns" went with me to see this interesting town. We passed through the old market place, then by a broad gravel walk to the top of this high rock, where stands this famous Sterling Castle, from which can be seen the battlefields where "Wallace fought for liberty and Robert Bruce secured his hard-won crown." From Victoria lookout and battlements the view of the surrounding country is magnificent, the tall mountain peaks in the Highlands, the valleys, and the stream winding through the meadows, is a picture that is photographed on my memory. History tells us that Sterling Castle dates back as a royal residence to A.D. 990, when Kenneth III. collected his forces there and marched to meet the Danes at Luncarty. It was the favorite residence of James V., and there James VI. spent his early years, under the tutorship of the celebrated George Buchanan. There are very many more historical facts connected with it which I would like to give. On the esplanade of the castle is a large statue representing King Robert Bruce sheathing his sword after the battle of Bannockburn. Leading up to the great arched doorway is a drawbridge over the dry fosse of the castle. There was a soldier pacing to and fro. I was much interested in going through this castle, which is strongly garrisoned. Mr. C—— proved to be an excellent guide, as he seemed quite familiar with the history of the castle. In one of the rooms there were a number of relics, which I spent some time inspecting. There were two old chairs, of the reigns of James III. and James V., respectively, and several old battle-axes found on the battlefield of Bannockburn, also a number of other rude weapons. In the Douglass room I saw a beautiful little window, put in by order of Queen Victoria to commemorate William Earl Douglass, murdered here in February, 1452, by James II. From the castle we went down a flight of stairs to a small garden, in the centre of which is a granite pyramid, erected to the memory of the Scottish covenanters by the late William Drummond, uncle of Professor Henry Drummond. It contains a number of Bible inscriptions, and in large, bold lettering these words: "Rock of Ages." The cemetery is on the slope a little below the castle, in what they call the valley. It is beautifully situated, and hundreds of Sterling's dead sleep there. In the centre are the statues of reformers Knox, Melville and Henderson, also a statue of the covenanting martyr Renwick, and one of James Guthrie, covenanting minister of the High Church, and martyr. There was a magnificent monument erected to the memory of the two young women who suffered a martyr's death. I copied the following inscription from this monument: "Margaret, virgin martyr of the ocean waves, with her like-minded sister Agnes, bound to a stake within flood mark of the Solway tide. They died a martyr's death May 11, 1685.

> "Love many waters cannot quench. God saves
> His chaste imperiled one in covenant true.
> Oh, Scotia's daughters, earnest scan the page
> And prize the flower blood bought for you."

There were a number of other beautiful inscriptions around the base of the monument. My pencil was busy copying epitaphs that attracted my attention which appear on the page set apart for them. We then visited the High Church, traditionally called the Church of the Grey Friars. The West Kirk, as it is called, was built in the fourteenth century, the East Kirk in the sixteenth century. This was the church that John Knox is said to have preached in. I saw the old pulpit and communion table that were in use then; they were on exhibition in Cowane's Hospital, commonly called Guildery. Over the doorway is the statue of John Cowane, one of the principal beneficiaries of the town. There were various curiosities, among which were old tankards, weights and measures that were used as standards.

TUESDAY, July 3 —I purposed leaving to-day for Glasgow to join Dr. R—— again, but Mr. J—— insisted so strongly on my remaining until I had visited all the principal places of interest in and around Sterling, that I took the risk of missing Dr. R—— and not having his company on my journey through Ireland. I visited the Wallace monument, which stands on a very high hill overlooking the river Forth. On the second floor of the tower is the armor of Wallace and busts of Sir Walter Scott, Carlyle, and William Murdock, inventor of lighting by gas; John Knox, born 1505, died 1572; Robert Burns and a number of others whose memories are cherished in Scotland and other countries; the sword used by King Robert Bruce at the battle of Sterling Bridge, September 11, 1297, with this inscription: "The sword fit for archangels to wield was light in his terrible hand." It was a long, tiresome journey to the top of the monument, but the view I had from the balcony more than repaid me for the exertion I made. The river Forth coursing its way in serpentine form through that fertile country, was a picture that no human hand could paint. I met a young man from Aberdeen, and together we went to the old Cambuskenneth Abbey. We paid twopence and secured the key from a family living in an old house a short distance away, and climbed up the winding stairway to the top of the abbey, which was crumbling with age, and from there we visited the tomb of James III., just back of the abbey. On our way to the ferry we stopped at a very old farmhouse and refreshed ourselves with a glass of milk. The floors of the old house were stone, and I should judge that the hand that placed them there had ceased from toil long years ago. When we reached the ferry we found a boy with a small rowboat ready to take us across the narrow stream, and a few strokes of the oar took us to the other side, the fare being a penny. I called at the Y. M. C. A. building and met the secretary, who is a merchant, and only gives his evenings to the work. I walked through a very pretty part of the city, the sidewalks in that section being about three feet above the centre of the street, and the grand old trees forming an arch over the whole, made it a beautiful sight. I saw the home of Professor Drummond's childhood, and it is a fine old residence. My friend, Mr. J——, was one of the Professor's Sunday school scholars, and he spoke very highly of him as a teacher.

Wednesday, July 4.—Mr. J—— described the beauties of the Trossachs to me and urged me to visit them, so I left for Callender on the 8 a. m. train, and from there rode on the top of a coach a distance of eight miles to the Trossachs; it was a delightful ride. The scenery was simply grand; the tall mountain peaks seemed to be lifting their heads in all directions, with here and there a beautiful sheet of water winding around their huge base. I sat on the seat with a fine old English gentleman and his wife, of Derbyshire, England, with whom I became quite well acquainted. Far up in the mountains we met two men with bag-pipes, and in company with them were two wretched looking women, each with young babes wrapped in shawls and strapped on their backs, in Indian style. The men walked down the road toward our coach and began discoursing a very peculiar air apparently for our benefit, but really for their own. We threw them some pennies and were glad to get beyond the discordant strains of their bag-pipes. Soon the Trossachs hotel hove in sight, from the top of which I saw the stars and stripes floating. I had been singing down in my heart all the morning, "The Star Spangled Banner," but as I caught sight of that old flag, I could scarcely keep that song I learned in childhood from finding its way to my lips. It being the celebration of our great Independence Day in America, the proprietor of this splendid hotel, alone far up in the highlands, had hoisted the flag in honor of his American guests and the American tourists passing through that section. We rode up to Loch Katrine and embarked on a little steamer for the head of that magnificent lake, which nestles between two mountains and is dotted with miniature islands. Ellen's Isle is a beautiful spot, mentioned by Scott in his poem entitled, "Lady of the Lake." In this romantic spot, amid the grandeur of this mountain scenery, the thoughts, the beauty of which have stirred the hearts of lovers of poetry in the old and new world, were suggested to Sir Walter Scott, the great poet. The ride up the lake is a beautiful one, the distance being nine miles. As our steamer sped along over the bosom of that placid lake, overshadowed by those lofty mountain peaks, it seemed almost like "fairy land." Most of the passengers were going to Glasgow by the Caledonian Canal, which the old English gentleman informed me was a trip well worth taking. There were a large number of American tourists waiting at the landing to take the steamer back to the Trossachs. They were very patriotic, judging from their display of the American flag, as most of the ladies had small flags festooned across their shoulders, and the gentlemen had them fastened to their umbrellas and canes, and they came on board the steamer apparently in the spirit of the day. I was not very long in making the fact known that I was born in the "Land of the free and home of the brave." But while this is the case, I also have a strong love for Old England and her three fair daughters, Ireland, Scotland and Wales. For in all my travels through the British Isles, from those living in luxury and wealth to those down in the "vale of poverty," I received nothing but kindness, and have every reason for believing that they have a good, warm feeling for America. I have always felt kindly toward strangers coming to our shores, but I think I shall feel more so in the future. Coming down the lake I had a grand view of Ben Venue, a grand old mountain whose tall peak seemed to be touching the clouds. It is 2,393 feet in height. Ben A'an can be seen lifting its rugged peak to the height of 1,851 feet. Then came our ride back to the hotel, in the rear of which is a mountain called Sron-Armailte, and is 1,149 feet in height. We remained there about an hour, giving us time to get some idea of the grandeur of the scenery. There were three coaches, and I rode from the steamer to the hotel on the small one, but concluded to find a seat on one of the others with the Americans, for there was only one man on the coach, and he sat with the driver, so when we were ready to leave for Callender I made an effort to get a seat on one of the other coaches, but was informed they were especially for the tourists, so I seated myself on top of the small coach for a quiet ride over the mountains, but just a few moments before leaving, two Catholic priests took seats beside me, one of them having the appearance of being about thirty-five years old, and the other about twenty-eight. I had no idea of forming their acquaintance, for I had never conversed with a priest. As we were about leaving, a man climbed up on the wheel and called for the driver's fee. When the priest sitting next to me passed him a shilling, he said: "I can't make the change."

I did not have a sixpence in change, so the priest said: "Just keep my shilling and consider this gentleman's fee paid," referring to me. I thanked him and told him I would give him the change when we reached Callender, but he replied, "I settled for you; I do not wish any change." We at once began a conversation, and I found them excellent company; they were jolly, good-natured men. We rode in the compartment together from Callender to Sterling. I was quite amused to hear the elder priest guy the younger one. They said to me: "Did you know we were priests?" "Oh, yes," I replied, and I thought when I saw you coming toward the coach I would have a quiet time of it going over the mountains." The elder one said: "You must have formed a very poor opinion of this gentleman," pointing to his companion. "I have formed a very good opinion of both of you," I replied, "and am very glad to have formed your acquaintance." We exchanged our religious views very pleasantly and when I was leaving them they grasped my hand, shook it warmly, and said: "We have spent a very pleasant afternoon with you." As this was the last night I expected to remain at Sterling, Mr. J—— invited to his house a number of his friends from Cambusbarron and Sterling, whom I had met, and a very enjoyable evening was spent. They sang some fine old Scotch airs for me, and then requested me to sing the "Star Spangled Banner." Just before they bade me a final adieu they sang, "Should Auld Acquaintance be Forgot," etc. I noted that evening as one of the most pleasant I spent during my stay in the old country.

THURSDAY, July 5.—I took my autoharp and went

to Cambusbarron and played and sang "In That City" for Mr. J——, Sr. I shall never forget that old man as he lay in bed with the tears coursing down his cheeks. Reaching out his hand to bid me goodbye, he said: "I shall never meet you here again, but will meet you in that "City," and then gave me a neatly folded little note, saying: "That contains my sentiments." As I passed out of the door of the little cottage I received the "God bless you!" from that family that I have numbered among my choice friends. In a letter received a short time ago from Mr. J—— came the information, "Father has gone to the eternal city that you sung to him about" When I returned to Sterling and bade good-bye to Mr. C—— and wife, Mr. J—— and his excellent wife and their six "wee bairns," a feeling of sadness crept over me as I thought that in all probability I am looking into the faces of these kind friends for the last time. Left the grand old town of Sterling at 1 P. M. and about an hour's ride brought me to the busy city of Glasgow, which has a population of about 800,000. History tells us that a small Roman colony once occupied this site, and about the year 560 St. Mungo founded a religious house here, so that it dates far back in the past. It is sixty miles from the sea, but is said to rival Liverpool in shipping. I passed over the splendid Glasgow bridge and was surprised to see the great number of ships lying at the docks far down the river. I promised my friends, Mr. and Mrs. S——, of Camden, New Jersey, that when I visited Glasgow I would call on their relatives. Mrs. S—— has a sister living at Paisley, a few miles from Glasgow, and thither I went by train. When I called on and informed her that I had a message from her sister in America she seemed overjoyed, as she had not heard from her for a number of years. She said: "It is nearly forty years since I bade her good-bye." I remained only a short time there and then rode on the top of a tram through one of the principal streets. The city has a magnificent town hall; the Coates cotton mill is an immense building; also passed the Coates Memorial Baptist Church, which is a large and handsome structure. On some of the business streets there were quite a number of large, well-stocked stores. The celebrated Paisley shawls are made here. Returned to Glasgow and called at the house of Mr. S—— 's sister, but they were away in the country. From there went to the Y. M. C. A. hall, and was directed by the assistant secretary to the Hotel Waverly, and found very comfortable quarters for the night.

FRIDAY, July 6.—Called at the Y. M. C. A. and met the secretary, Mr. O——, and found him one of the brightest and most genial secretaries that I met during my travels. When he learned I was the author of the hymn, "A Sinner Like Me," he informed me that his wife, who is the daughter of the Rev. Horatius Bonar, the celebrated hymn writer, had been singing that hymn all over Scotland as a solo for a number of years, and he said: "I am sure she would be pleased to meet you, and as she is to meet a committee of ladies at the Young Women's Christian Association Hall in a short time, I will take you around and introduce you." And so we went to this fine hall fitted up for young ladies, which reflects great credit on the people of Glasgow, and met this distinguished lady, along with a number of others of Scotland's noted Christian women. The Y. M. C. A. hall is one of the largest and best equipped that I visited. Mr. O—— kindly gave me a plan whereby I could see the principal places of interest. The municipal building is a very large and handsome structure, and is an ornament to the city. The stores on Buchanan street, which is one of the principal thoroughfares, compare favorably with any city on either side of the Atlantic. The old Cathedral interested me very much and I spent considerable time there. The large stained glass windows are magnificent, and the designs on them attracted my attention. The dimensions given of the old edifice are 319 feet long and 63 feet wide. It contains a number of pieces of statuary and tablets, and the old churchyard is filled with slabs with inscriptions that can scarcely be read, being so old. Back of the Cathedral, terraced on the side of the hill, is a beautiful cemetery in which stands the monument of Knox and a number of others of Scotland's cherished dead. I also visited West End, where there are a number of elegant residences, the Botanical Gardens, the University, and a finely arranged park claimed my attention for a short time. I embarked on the steamer "Shamrock" for Londonderry, Ireland, and had a good view of the shipyards as we passed down the river Clyde. It was one continuous sound of the hammer until we got beyond the city limits. A severe thunder storm poured its fury out upon us when we were a little below the city, so that I was deprived of a good view of the scenery along the river. We reached Greenoch at 6:30 and then started seaward again. I left Scotland charmed with its beauties, and shall always kindly remember her warm-hearted and hospitable people.

A Trip Through "Old Ireland."

SATURDAY, July 7.—When I came out on deck we were steaming up the river Foyle and the scenery was charming. Those great hills, sloping down to the margin of the river dotted with little farm-houses, was very picturesque, and as we approached Londonderry it struck me as being a very pretty little city. It is built on both sides of the river; on what is called Water Side, the houses seemed to be terraced on the side of the hill, and a handsome bridge spans the river just above where we landed. When I stepped ashore I could scarcely realize I was in "Old Ireland," a land I have always desired to see. A young man from Australia, with whom I became acquainted on the steamer, had some business to attend to and invited me to go with him. We crossed in a miniature ferry-boat, which was an odd-looking craft, and returned by way of the bridge to the city proper. The old walls that still surround the city and are preserved as a promenade, were built in 1688 and some parts of them bear the marks of the bullets made during the wonderful siege of 'Derry. I walked around them and had a good view of the city. I saw the large cannon called "Roaring Meg," used during the siege. Londonderry has a population of about 35,000, and the business portion compares favorably with any city of its size that I visited. Some of the "shops" are quite large. I called at the Y. M. C. A. and at the postoffice, thinking I might find some trace of Dr. R——, but failed to do so. My old heart bounded with joy when they passed me out some mail matter from America, forwarded to me by my good friend, Mrs. P——, of Harborn, England. I was alone in a strange land, and as I read those letters I felt that I was in close touch with those who had kindly written them. I went to the old cathedral and the lady having charge kindly showed me through, and before I left, called my attention to an old cannon ball found in the yard after the siege. I called at the manse (or parsonage) of the East Wall Wesleyan Church and introduced myself to the pastor, Rev. Mr. O——, and found him a good, warm-hearted old gentleman. After some conversation he invited me to preach for him on Sunday morning. I thanked him and told him when I preached I generally had a very small congregation—no one there but Butler. He smiled and said: "Oh, I thought you were a preacher." He requested me to help him in his service in the morning and evening, and directed me to one of his members who kept a temperance hotel, which I found to be a very homelike place. Went down through a part of the city containing a number of little houses, one of which, with its little windows, amused me particularly. I saw a typical old Irish woman sitting in the market-place smoking a clay pipe, seemingly getting a great deal of comfort from it. The Salvation Army made quite a display, and held a very excellent service on one of the principal streets. I was compelled to take refuge from the storm in a large grocery store, and one of the gentlemen, who thought me a native of Ireland, became quite friendly and invited me to call in whenever I was in that locality. I had about walked the soles off my shoes and called at a cobbler's shop, and while they were being repaired had quite an interesting conversation with the proprietor. The old man was quite interested in my description of America. Before I retired I began to feel somewhat at home in "Old Ireland."

SUNDAY, July 8.—According to promise, I was present at service at the East Wall Wesleyan Church, and assisted the pastor as best I could : in the afternoon went to the Sabbath school and addressed the children. Mr. A——, the assistant superintendent, who had charge of the school, had a large, warm Irish heart in him, and made me feel quite at home in their presence. In the evening I took charge of the prayer service after the sermon, as the pastor had to go over to the Water Side and preach at another chapel. I became acquainted with quite a number of the members, among them a Mr. McC—— and a Mr. H——, the latter gentleman formerly from the town of Tipperary, which is in the south of Ireland. He urged me to visit his old home when I was in that locality. When I returned to the hotel I found several persons who had just landed from the steamer "City of Rome." They had been living in America for a number of years, and had returned to the home of their childhood on a visit. Mr. B——, the proprietor, introduced me to them as being from America, and they, thinking I was formerly from the "Old Sod," said to me: "How long has it been since you left

8

Ireland?" "Indeed," I said, "I have never left yet." They looked surprised, and in reply said: "We understood the gentleman to say your home was in America." "So it is," I replied; "but I have never left Ireland, for the reason I never was here before." They smiled, and said: "We thought you were an Irishman." My grandmother Butler's father came from the north of Ireland, so I concluded that I must resemble him in a very striking manner, and according to her discription of him, I am quite willing it should be so.

MONDAY, July 9.—Left 'Derry for Port Rush on the 8 A. M. train. In the same compartment as myself were several Americans. I engaged in conversation with them, and, when they informed me they were from Wilmington, Delaware, I felt as though I had met friends almost directly from home. Port Rush is a seaside resort, and from what I could see of it in passing through on the train, I jotted it down in my note book as a very pretty little town. From Port Rush I rode on the electric tram to Giant's Causeway. We ran very close along the wild, rocky coast, and I kept my eyes busy gazing at those strange looking caverns formed in the white rocks. The ruins of Dunluce Castle, on a rock about 100 feet above the sea, attracted my attention, and I felt inclined to leave the tram and explore the old ruins. A narrow wall connects the castle with the mainland. Giant's Causeway is a marvelous formation of rocks. One would think surely they were chiseled out by human hands and placed there. Most of the stones were quite uniform, and, as far as I can recollect, they were something over one foot in diameter, perfectly level on top, and a few inches apart, reminding one of stepping-stones. My description of the size of the stones may not be accurate; had I then had any idea of publishing my diary, I would have made more elaborate notes of this wonderful place. The Causeway extends a short distance out into the sea. I sat on those rocks, with the waves breaking gently at their base, and wrote in my note book. There are formations bearing different names in the rocks in and around the Causeway. "The Giant's Gateway," "Giant's Organ," "Chimney Tops," "The Priest and His Flock," and "The Hen and Chickens" were some of the titles given them. In order to see everything of interest here, it is necessary to go with a guide in his small boat. This I did not do, for the clouds hung low and occasionally dropped down great sheets of water, compelling me to hurriedly find a refuge. I met an old lady selling photographs of the Causeway and little trinkets. I purchased some articles of her, and when she urged me to continue in the good work, I informed her I had used up all my small change. She gave me her blessing, and looked up into my face and said, with her good, rich brogue: "It's meself thot had a good mon, an' as foine a lookin' b'y as ye" (I thought the old lady's eyes needed attention when she called me a boy), "thot wint out to sea an' niver come back; thot's why I'm carryin' this basket." After failing to respond to her pathetic appeal, she concluded I must, indeed, be short of change. In going out on the Causeway again, I saw a group of old ladies with their baskets of wares, the same old lady being one of

the number. They were standing near what is called
the "Wishing Chair," a stone with several others
a trifle smaller encircling it. These old ladies were
anxious that I should sit on it; one of them in particular assuring me that if I made three wishes while
sitting there they would surely come true. I knew she
was talking for a shilling, and the old lady whom I
had met before helped me out by saying: "Don't be
botherin' him; he's no change; he spint it with me."
But she paid no attention to what No. 1 said, but kept
saying to me: "Sit ye down;" so I finally consented.
They gathered around me and insisted that I should
make three wishes before I arose. I told them I had
only one wish, and that was to get up, for it was wet
down there, and that wish came true, for I was soon
on my feet. They were all talking at a very rapid
rate, and I said to them as I was leaving: "Well,
peace to your bones." A man who was standing near
said: "What bones do you mean, jaw bones?" I left
Giant's Causeway well pleased with my visit there,
and if any of the readers should visit that beautiful
island across the sea, do not fail to see Giant's Causeway. When I returned to Londonderry, I met Mr.
McC—— and Mr. H——, and we took a walk on the
Water Side, along the embankment on the river
front, and, as we ascended the hill, had a good view of
'Derry. This is a very romantic place; we could see
far over into County Donegal. I met the Rev. Mr.
Q—— again, and his good wife, and bade them a final
adieu as I was to leave in the morning, and called on
several with whom I had so pleasantly associated
during the few days I spent in their city. Mr.

McC—— and my Tipperary friend spent the evening with me at the hotel. I regretted leaving Londonderry so soon, and I shall always remember my visit there with pleasure.

TUESDAY, July 10.—I arose early and "booked" for Belfast. Mr. McC——, who is a traveling salesman for a large business house in Londonderry, met me at the train and rode with me as far as one of the towns in County Donegal. The Donegal whiskers I have heard spoken of quite often, but here I saw the genuine article. A little man boarded the train at one of the stations in County Donegal; his hair was a bright red and his whiskers were a shade *redder*; they began a little below his ears, encircling his throat, and made a very striking border for his collar. He sat opposite me, and I had to suppress a laugh, which was quite an effort for me to do. At Omagh, the county seat of Tyrone, I "broke my journey." I have some friends who lived there at one time, and have heard them speak of Omagh so frequently that as I walked through the streets of that pleasant little town it seemed quite familiar to me. The county court was about convening, and, judging from the crowd that were in and about the court-house, business was brisk. I saw the lawyers hurrying to and fro with documents in their hands, preparing to untangle some unfortunate one from the meshes of the law. In traveling through the different countries I found old human nature about the same. Prisons and court-houses are just as necessary over there as they are in our great country. The great adversary is succeeding all too well in making men and women believe that his way is the best. I took the liberty of calling on the Rev. Mr. F——, pastor of the Wesleyan Chapel, who gave me a cordial reception, and expressed his regrets at my not being able to be with him on Sunday. He pointed out the old manse (or parsonage) where one of my friends lived when a young lady, her father being pastor of the chapel at that time. They were erecting a very large Catholic church and it struck me that money was not so hard to get hold of there as I had imagined, judging from the number of fine churches of different denominations, and the amount of business the merchants seemed to be doing. I visited the poor district, and was interested in the miniature houses, in which the occupants seemed to be perfectly happy. Left for Belfast in the afternoon, passing through Duncannon, which is quite a large town. We changed cars at Portadown, then passed through the towns of Moy, Lurgan and Lisburn. Some of these towns are noted for the manufacture of fine linen. We passed a number of bogs where men and women were engaged in digging and piling up the peat, which they cut into small squares and pile up to dry. It is used as fuel by a great many of the people. I asked an old man, who had a cartload for sale in Omagh, for a piece of it. "Help yourself to all you want," he said. After a ride of something over four hours I arrived at Belfast, a city that I felt at home in as soon as I entered, it seemed so Americanlike in its appearance. It has a population of about 260,000, is nicely laid out, and one can find their way about as easily as in our own great city of Philadelphia. The large stores that lined the principal business streets (the proprietors of which seemed to be as full of snap and push as any wide-awake merchant in America) were wonderfully attractive, and most of them were well patronized by the ladies, who seemed to be spending their shillings as rapidly as the average American lady disposes of her husband's extra change. As is my custom, I made my way to the Y. M. C. A. hall, an organization that every city and town should have, and that all Christian and good-thinking people should be interested in. Hundreds of young men have been saved from being wrecked, and a host more might be if more attention was given to this very worthy institution, and the churches would be all the stronger by the grand work done by these associations. On going into a strange city, alone especially, a feeling of loneliness would take possession of me, but when I saw the sign of the Y. M. C. A. on a building, and entered, I always found the secretary or his assistant ready to give me a warm shake of the hand and bid me feel at home, and frequently I have formed the acquaintance of those whose company has been very helpful to me. These places are open when the churches are not. I was directed at the hall to a temperance hotel on East College Square, and, like most of the places I stopped at, was very homelike. At the hall in the evening I met a Mr. F——, a very excellent young man, formerly from Edinburgh, Scotland, who was preparing himself for mission work in Africa. His life was rather a sad one, his father being dead, and his mother had lost her reason beyond recovery.

WEDNESDAY, July 11.—By my note book I see the day was spent in a general tramp around the city.

Went out nearly to Cave Hill, and in coming back saw a group of people gathered around a large church waiting to catch a glimpse of a young couple who were having the nuptial knot tied, and I thought there was about as much curiosity manifested as I had ever seen over in America on such occasions. It seemed to be a day set apart for performing that ceremony, for a little beyond, in front of another church, was another large crowd, anxiously waiting to see the fresh bride and groom. On visiting the docks, found the shipping was quite extensive, and shipbuilding is carried on here on a large scale, a number of large vessels plying between Liverpool and New York having been built here. Went through a very old and odd-looking market. It seemed to me that I was paying a visit to Noah's ark; one could, for a few shillings, purchase goods enough to begin housekeeping on a small scale. Also visited a part of the city containing a great many handsome residences, and from there went to the district of the working class; most of the houses were two-story brick, and were very comfortable looking homes. While on the top of a tram, riding through the principal business streets, I met two gentlemen from Baltimore, Maryland, who asked me a question about a certain place we were passing, and when I informed them I was from America, they said: "We thought you were a resident here." A short time afterward, while in Robinson & Cleaver's immense dry goods store making some purchases, the clerk waiting on me said: "I should judge from your appearance you were a native of our country." This store is the largest and finest in Belfast, and is noted for its cheap and elegant linens. On returning to the Y. M. C. A. hall, met Mr. B——, the secretary, whom I had heard speak at Exeter Hall, London. He, like myself, is a bachelor with several years piled up on him. He introduced me to Rev. Mr. McA——, who informed me that he had visited America, and his wife was formerly from Wayne, Pennsylvania. Mr. B—— asked me if I was married. Of course I answered no. The reverend gentleman said, with a great deal of humor, "you ought to have known he was a bachelor by his sad looking countenance." In reply, I said: "We are the ones that possess sunshine, notwithstanding public opinion is against us."

THURSDAY, July 12.—This was a general holiday in Belfast, it being the annual celebration of Orangemen. The Y. M. C. A. made an excursion to the Isle of Man, taking about 1,500. The Orangemen had a very large parade; some part of it formed on East College Square, and the entire procession passed within a block of the hotel, so I saw most of it from my window. The brass bands were quite numerous, and most of them were very good. There was a very elaborate display of banners all over the city; even in the small streets they were stretched across from the houses on the opposite side. In the afternoon, took a ride to Balmoral, about one mile from where the celebration took place. Two young men, who I met on the tram, walked with me through a beautiful part of the country, and on our return we met the parade on the homeward march. Aside from a few who had been keeping company with "John Barleycorn," they were very orderly. The whole thing, both in and out of the city, passed off quietly. The young men went with me to the Dublin boat, in which I embarked for the city of Dublin. There were very few passengers, and the steamer was small and the accommodations poor, but as my shillings were getting short and I could save several by going that way, I concluded I would endure it for one night. I formed the acquaintance of a medical student; he was a bright, interesting fellow, and we passed the evening very pleasantly together. Had a good view of the sea front of County Antrim and County Down, as we passed along in the steamer.

FRIDAY, July 13.—The ride up River Liffey, which divides the grand old city of Dublin, with its 420,000 inhabitants, was a pleasant one. We landed about 6:30 A. M. There were very few people on the streets, and scarcely any business houses open. As a rule, they begin business between the hours of 8 and 9 A. M. Some of the smaller places are ready for trade about 7 o'clock. Near the Quay, where we landed, I saw an old lady that quite amused me; she had a basket of fruit, and was sitting in the bottom of a cart. She had on a large pair of shoes that stood up like monuments, and a little, old-fashioned black bonnet relieved by a white cap peeping out from it, with three frills, the last one encircling a very decided looking face. After bidding Mr. W——, the medical student, adieu, I was alone again in a strange city. A short walk from the Quay brought me to Sackeville street, one of the principal thoroughfares, and which is a beautiful street. A great many of the stores, both in this and other business streets, are quite as fine as most of the London stores. After taking a stroll down this street and over the O'Connell Bridge to Trinity College and the Bank of Ireland, I inquired the way to the Y. M. C. A. hall, and was directed there, it being on Lower Abbey street, a short distance from Sackeville street. Left my luggage there, and sallied forth to see another part of the city, passing through Marlborough street, on which is a large cathedral, and back to Sackville street, where stands Nelson's monument, which is 121 feet high. A sixpence, the attendant informed me, would admit me, which amount I paid, and climbed the winding stairway to the balcony, from which I had a good view of the city and surrounding country. The Hill of Howth, the Irish Sea, the Wicklow Mountains, the beautiful country, and most of the city was scenery that I considered very fine. On returning from the monument to the Y. M. C. A. hall, I met the secretary, Mr. W—— B——, a warm-hearted, genial man, whose bright, cheerful face I shall not soon forget, and whose kind deeds, along with those of whom I met through him, I have hung on memory's wall, to remain through all the years of my life. He gave me such a cordial welcome I almost felt I was meeting an old friend. He introduced me to the secretary of the City Union, and he at once invited me to address the Sunday Morning Breakfast, as the gentleman who was to speak had disappointed them. "If I am large enough to fill the breach," I said, "you can use me." I presume he concluded if I possessed ability according to my size, I would answer very well. Mr. B—— took me to a temperance hotel on Lower Abbey street, kept by Mrs. E——, a remarkably fine, motherly old lady, where I remained during my stay in Dublin. As Mr. B—— and I were coming down Sackeville street, we met a Mr. H——, to whom I was introduced. He was a young man whose ready wit could not be surpassed. The witty remarks that he and Mr. B—— passed out to each other caused me to laugh so that I attracted the attention of the passersby. The Ladies' Auxiliary of the Y. M. C. A. were to give a tea party at the Hill of Howth, on Saturday afternoon, and Mr. B—— invited me to go along, and as he had to go with the ladies in the morning to assist them, he requested Mr. H—— to meet me at the hall at a given time in the afternoon, and pilot me to Howth, which he readily agreed to do. Mr. B—— invited me to go with him to Kingstown, a few miles from Dublin, where he boarded, he being a bachelor also, although not quite so far advanced as myself. A half hour's ride brought us to his home, which was near the sea wall, and from the window where I sat I had a good view of the Irish Sea, which behaves so badly at times. His roommate, a Mr. S——, was a pleasant young Englishman and very entertaining. The lady of the house was a kind, hospitable woman and a strict member of the Roman Catholic Church. She was interested in hearing about America, as she had two sons living in Brooklyn, New York. I was introduced to a Mr. McC—— and family living near by, a gentleman holding a position in the Dublin postoffice. He invited us to take supper with him. I wondered how I would manage another meal after such a one as this good lady had prepared for us. After returning from a long walk, we sat down to a table laden with tempting food, and I succeeded grandly in hiding considerable of it away. It was very late when I returned to Dublin. Mr. B —— informed me the train would stop a short distance from Lower Abbey street, but the guard said this was the last train for the night, and did not go beyond the main station, which was a long distance from my hotel. I fastened my eye on a very respectable looking young man who was coming from the train, and finally asked him to direct me to Lower Abbey street; he said: "I am going in that vicinity, and will accompany you." He gained my confidence, and I felt quite safe with him as we wended our way through what seemed to be a rough locality. I thanked him kindly as he left me at the door, and put him on the long list of warm-hearted Irishmen.

SATURDAY, July 14.—I joined Secretary B—— and a young man whom I afterward learned was employed in the same store with my friend W——, at Cheapside, London, and we were shown through the Bank of Ireland, through the courtesy of a friend of Mr. B——, who holds a position of trust there. It is customary to clip the bank notes when they are returned, as they are used but once. I gathered up a few of the clippings, and had a great desire to gather up some of the notes, legitimately, as my roll was getting exceedingly small. After leaving the bank the young man from London and I visited the Glasvevin Cemetery, where rests the remains of Daniel O'Connell, whose memory is cherished by Irishmen the world over. We each paid a sixpence and went down into the vault and saw his coffin, with those of other members of his family; also visited the grave of Parnell, and saw a young lady forming the letters of his name on the mound with fresh cut flowers. There were a number of wreaths in immortelles, placed there by different societies. We saw a number of fine monuments, erected to the memory of other prominent men of Ireland, some of whom had been bishops of the Roman Catholic Church. Leaving the quiet resting place of the dead, we came through a new and very pretty part of the city, where the young man left me to take the train for home. After leaving him I went through Moore street, which was so crowded with people marketing that quite often I had to walk in the centre of the street. The vegetables looked very nice, although there was not such a variety as we see displayed in our markets. Met Mr. H—— at the appointed time and place, and asked him whether it would be advisable for us to go to the Hill of Howth, as it was then raining. He replied in a manner which made me laugh heartily : " You are in a strange kind of a country now ; Howth is nine miles away, and it may not be raining there. Sometimes it rains on one side of Sackeville street and is dry on the other." "Then we will go," I replied, " if that is the kind of climate you have in Ireland." We were joined at the Amein Street Station by a number of good, jolly young men. Several of them in our compartment were inclined to guy Mr. H——, but he always had an answer ready to pass out to them. One young man, sitting opposite me, noticed Mr. H——'s handkerchief showing from his coat pocket and said to him : " H——, I think I have seen that handkerchief before." Scarcely had he finished the sentence when Mr. H—— said : " It is quite likely, for your poor old mother washed for me three weeks ago." The manner in which he made this remark caused a roar of laughter, even the young man, although somewhat confused, joining in the laugh. We did very little but laugh at the wit of Mr. H——; who was formerly from the city of Cork. On reaching Howth, which is a good sized town, we walked through a splendid domain to a beautiful spot, where the ladies had prepared lunch for us. There were about fifty persons in the company, men and women of culture and refinement, most of whom were actively engaged in Christian work. I was introduced by Mr. B—— to the entire company, and requested to sing the hymn I have so often referred to, it being a favorite of most of them. Among the number was the Rev. Mr. K—— and wife. Mr. K—— is a prominent Presbyterian minister of Belfast, and, I was informed, is a man whose influence for good is widespread. I had a pleasant conversation with him and his excellent wife. Mr. F——, who is one of Dublin's successful merchants, invited me to spend Sunday with him at his home, near Donneybrook, a suburb of Dublin. Mr. B—— told me it was in all order to accept the invitation. Then a Mr. W—— came to me and invited me to his home at Black Rock, another of Dublin's beautiful suburban towns. I told him I had planned to go to the Lakes of Killarney on Monday, but he insisted on me postponing my trip and pay him a visit on Monday, which I finally consented to, and shall never regret having done so. One of the gentlemen photographed the entire party, and afterward a small group, in which my tall form is quite conspicuous.

We climbed to the peak of the grand old Hill of Howth, which overlooks the Irish Sea, and from which can be seen Ireland's Eye and Kingstown harbor, and the sea front of County Wicklow. Before leaving the grounds the Rev. Mr. K—— gave us a very good address, after which Mrs. F—— rendered a solo that was highly appreciated. She has a sweet, musical voice. That afternoon spent at the Hill of Howth, with those who showed me, the tall stranger, so much kindness and attention, I shall always look back to with very pleasant recollections.

SUNDAY, July 15.—According to previous engagement I went to the Y. M. C. A. hall at 8 A. M. to address the Sunday Morning Breakfast. There were something over 600 men and women assembled, who, judging from their appearance, came from the slums of the city. I did my best to throw out the "Life Line" to those unfortunate ones, and trust that some one was rescued by my effort. From there went to Merion Hall, where the Plymouth Brethren, of which Mr. and Mrs. F—— are members, hold their services. I attended the bread-breaking, which is the first service, and then listened to a very excellent sermon by a minister from a distant town. Mr. F——, having to take charge of his father's mission at one of the suburban towns, was unable to meet me at the hall, so he had arranged that I should accompany his wife to their home. A half hour's walk brought us to their elegant residence, at Donneybrook, where I was royally entertained. Mrs. F—— introduced me to her two little daughters, one six and the other eight years old. They gave me a reception I shall never forget;

they threw their little arms around my neck, saying: "Welcome to our home, Mr. Butler." I was relating this incident in the home of a friend in Pennsylvania, where there were a number of young ladies present. One of them excused herself for interrupting and said: "Mr. Butler, if you were expecting to be treated in like manner by the young ladies here this evening, we have been rather slow in performing our duty." The story ended in a grand laugh, in which none joined more heartily than myself. The long walk to the home of Mr. F—— prepared me to do justice to the sumptuous meal awaiting me. It was so entirely homelike it did not seem like my first visit there. The little girls were remarkably bright and interesting, and sang beautifully with their mother. Mr. F——, who came home shortly after our arrival there, gave me an account of their mission work. They insisted on my remaining with them to tea, as the secretary, Mr. B——, was expected there, which I did, returning with Mr. B—— in time for the evening service at the Y. M. C. A. hall. Secretary B——, who is very earnest in his efforts to rescue the lost, has a noble band of young men who assist him in his good work.

MONDAY, July 16.—In company with Mr. B——, went to the Dublin Visiting Medical Mission. This very worthy institution was recently organized by some of the charitably disposed persons of Dublin. It is nonsectarian, and is supported entirely by the liberality of the people. Mr. B—— is one of the committee, and Mrs. F—— one of the secretaries. Many of the poor in the courts and alleys of Dublin know Mrs. F——, not simply from her passing their door, but from her visits to their wretched homes, and remember her kindly for administering to their needs. They have a short service in the mission rooms prior to the dispensing of medicines. There were about forty persons present, who evidently felt the pinching of poverty, some of them having very sad looking countenances. They listened attentively to the speaker as he told them of the Great Physician who could cure their sin-sick souls. At the close of the service they received treatment from Dr. F——, a young man, whom I was informed was an excellent Christian. In coming from the mission we passed through some of the slums, for Dublin, like every other city in the world, has its sections where the degraded congregate. In the afternoon went to Black Rock, a short distance from the city, where Mr. J—— W—— resides, one of the gentlemen I met at Howth on Saturday. On entering that fine, large home I received another good old Irish welcome. Mr. W—— and his wife and two sons and daughter, and his sister, made me feel at once that I was with friends, and not strangers. Miss W——, who is an accomplished young lady, and her brother, played several fine duets on the piano. Both of the sons are graduates of Trinity College, Dublin. Mr. W—— informed me that his brother, living at Howth, had sent me an invitation to visit and take dinner with him on Tuesday. My plans were arranged to go to the south of Ireland, and having already delayed my trip for a visit to this home, thought I must be on the move early on Tuesday, but Mr. W—— had a way of putting things that made you think his way was the best; he planned to have me call at his place of business, and, with his youngest son, visit some places of interest that I had not yet seen, and afterwards meet him at the Amein Street Station at a given time and he would accompany me to Howth. So passed another pleasant evening in one of Old Ireland's many refined Christian homes.

TUESDAY, July 17.—While in the vicinity of Stephen's Green it began raining very hard. Stepping into a music store for shelter, to my surprise I found one of the firm was a young man whom I had met at the picnic at Howth. After the rain ceased I took a stroll through a number of beautiful streets that I had not visited before, and on which were many grand homes. Dublin is considered a very wealthy city. Paid a hurried visit to Phœnix Park, for the clouds gave me warning that they would soon begin business again. It is no trouble to rain in Ireland. Near one of the monuments I found an old coin; the date on it was 1689. In the park I met a young man who had a strong desire to go to America, but I think before I left him I had convinced him he was better off in Ireland, for the present. At the Corn Exchange, where Mr. W——'s place of business is, I met his son, and together we went through old Trinity College, from which have gone many young men who have been an honor to Old Ireland. We spent some time in the Museum and in the National Art Gallery. There were a number of Ireland's old relics in the former place. I came away much pleased with my visit to these places of interest. Rode out to the suburbs of the city, then walked to the village of Rathfarnham, then went to Amein Street Station and met Mr. W——

and his brother and niece, and a short ride brought us to
Howth. Rode from the station in an Irish jaunting
car; they sat on the seat without any effort, apparently,
but I tightly grasped the arm of the seat and wondered
even then whether or not I would find myself rolling in
the dust. Mr. W——'s home stands upon the hill,
from which can be had a good view of the sea, and for
grandeur it compares with any that I visited.
We took a walk along the high bluff, where, far below,
breakers were dashing at its base. They showed me the
spot where a few weeks previous an English tourist fell
over the cliff and lodged on a ledge of rocks some
distance below, where he was found some hours afterward, badly injured, and was rescued with great
difficulty. As I gathered around the table with Mr.
W——'s family, which consisted of his wife, two
daughters and two sons. I concluded I had not met a
more refined and hospitable family.

WEDNESDAY, July 18.—The train left King's
Bridge Station at 7 A. M. for Killarney, and I was compelled to walk the long distance to the station, as there
were no trams running at that hour, for I presume
there is not traffic enough to pay much earlier than 7
o'clock. The country from Dublin to Killarney is
very beautiful, but I noticed that comparatively small
portions of it were under cultivation. In the compartment with me were an old Scotch lady and her son
and daughter. I soon managed to get into conversation with them. The gentleman informed me they
had been to America, most of their time being spent in
the West. They considered America a great country.
It was a journey of about seven hours from Dublin to

Killarney, and the interesting conversation I had with these Scotch people, together with the beautiful scenery, made it very pleasant. The town of Killarney, with a population of about 5,000, aside from a few large hotels and a cathedral, is not very inviting. I was surprised, on entering the town, to find so many small and wretched looking houses, but the sublime scenery all about it any lover of nature would not soon weary of. A young man in Dublin referred me to a hotel kept by a Mrs. J——. Just as I arrived she said: "There are two jaunting cars about leaving for the lakes, and there is room on the rear car for you if you wish to go." As I intended to remain only until the next morning, I availed myself of the opportunity of taking in the grandeur of that lake region, which any one visiting Ireland should not fail to see. There were three Americans and an Irishman and his son, from Glasgow, on one car, while on the other was his wife and daughter and sister-in-law. As I seated myself beside his wife, he got off the car and came over to me and said: "That is my wife; see that you do not run off with her." In reply I said: "I have no wife of my own, and you need have no fear of me depriving you of yours." Our driver was wit boiled down. He was a young man, and the lady sitting next to me called him, in a familiar way, "Bill." He drove his fine animal quite briskly, and I bounced about on the seat, and felt a little uncertain whether I would stay there or not, with all my holding on. I asked him whether he had any shoemakers' wax, to which he replied, in the broadest Irish I had heard in all my travels, "What does yez want with that?" "To put on the seat," I replied, "for I shall not be able to stay much longer, at the rate you are driving." "Shoemaker's wax we've not," he said, "but it's cobbler's we have." We had not proceeded far before it began to rain, "Let me off," I said, "I will go back to the hotel; I don't care to go any further in the rain." "Sit yez still; it is nothin' but the prasperation comin' from the mountain," he said, in a way that caused me to laugh so loud they heard me on the other car, though some distance away. Then he and the lady carried on a conversation that called forth one continuous roar of laughter. "You could make your living in America very nicely," I said to him. "What at, lying?" the lady remarked. "Well," said he, "If they were as well pleased with a lie as with the truth, and paid me for it, what would be the difference?" I said to him, after I had partly ceased laughing, "There's a heap in that head of yours." "Yes," said he, "more than yez would be knockin' out with a comb." The rain ceased about as quickly as it commenced, and we drove to the gate of a large domain, attended by an old man, who insisted upon our paying him a certain amount for allowing us to go through, but, after a long and heated debate between him and the parties on the head car, we were allowed to pass through for considerable less. The drive was delightful through this fine estate to Muckross Abbey. From my pocket guide book I learned the ruins were a church and abbey founded 1440, and partly rebuilt in 1602, and is yet in a fairly good condition; in the enclosure of these old ruins were several very ancient looking tombs. I stood on five of them, beneath which, I was informed, the five kings of Ireland were buried. We remained some time at this interesting old place; leaving here, we rode along a fine driveway overlooking a lake lying between the mountains. One would have to see the scenery here to appreciate its grandeur; words are inadequate to describe it. We stopped at an old cave, the entire party, with the exception of myself, going through. The entrance was small, and the exit much smaller, so I contented myself with merely looking in, and concluded not to enter the gloomy cavern, for it might be rather trying on my clothing as well as on my huge frame. "Bill" called out and said: "Are you not going in?" "No," I replied, "not a foot of me; my bones will be in a place like that soon enough." He, with his ready wit, said: "Ah, there is a way out of that, though there'll not be out of the grave." We rode along the mountain side until we came to a quaint old house, and then left the jaunting cars and crossed a ravine, down which a little sparkling stream came tumbling over the rocks and formed a small waterfall near where we passed. We climbed up the side of the mountain and gained the top, and with great delight "viewed the landscape o'er," and I am sure my eyes never rested on grander scenery. The Irish gentleman pointed out the spot where a tourist had, only a short time previous, ventured too near the precipice and was crushed on the rocks several hundred feet below. I kept my distance, for I was anxious to again see old friends in America. Just before "Bill" and the other driver turned their horses' heads homeward, this same Irish gentleman, who seemed familiar with that section of the country, and with the ways of the people, especially the drivers, came around to each one for a fee for " Bill " and his partner. Our bundle of wit said: "This is our harvest; there is nothing left us here in the winter, but the fireside and the lunatic asylum; I generally go to the asylum." When I returned to the hotel and paid the few shillings for that enjoyable ride, I considered it money well spent. " Bill " and the Lakes of Killarney are indelibly impressed on my memory. I took a walk through the main streets, stopped in one of the stores and purchased a blackthorn cane, which I brought to America.

THURSDAY, July 19.—Went by early train to Malloy, and from there to the city of Cork. I was curious to see the old city, having heard so much about it. In passing through its streets, it impressed me as being a very busy place, although there are comparatively few manufacturing places there. It has a population of about 80,000, and has a number of very good business thoroughfares. It was market day, and the streets were filled with people buying and selling. Most of the market women looked as though they belonged back in the long-ago. They wore ancient looking bonnets with white caps, whose frills were conspicuous. Some of them were apparently very fond of their clay pipes. The little donkeys, overshadowed by carts loaded with produce, amused me. Was directed by a policeman to the Y. M. C. A. hall. The secretary, Mr. B——, showed me through the building, which is one of the best equipped halls that I have ever been in. They have a fine gymnasium, and quite a large audience-room. Mr. B—— introduced me to

Mr. George W——, who organized the outdoor meetings in Cork, and who has been subject to so much persecution from some of the rough element of the city. While at the hall, met a number of good, sociable men and engaged in a pleasant conversation with them, which gave me a homelike feeling. One of them was a professor of music, and seemed to be a perfect master of the organ. On coming from the hall, heard a brass band discoursing a fine air, and on reaching one of the main streets, found it on the lead of a large circus parade, which had drawn the people from far and near, for the streets were thronged; and children! well, from the vast number that were following the parade I concluded that Ireland, even though she had furnished America with a good portion of her population, would be well able to keep up her record. The clerk who waited on me in a store where I made some purchases said, as I used an expression familiar only in America, "I thought you were a native of our country until I heard you express yourself just now;" and so from Londonderry to Cork they claimed that if I did live in America, I was born in Ireland. As I traveled through this beautiful island and mingled with her people, I concluded that no one need hesitate to acknowledge coming from such a grand country. In passing along St. Patrick street, saw the statue of Father Matthews, a man who was very earnest in the great cause of temperance. Went to St. Ann's Church, built 1722, and which has a spire 120 feet high; it is said to be one of the most interesting churches in Cork; it was crowded with devout worshippers. The cathedral of St. Fionn Bar is a large and beautiful structure.

I wrote my name in the record book, then leisurely walked through the cathedral and greatly admired its beauty, especially the altar. On coming out, met a Catholic priest on the opposite side of the street, and remarked to him: "That is a fine structure; I thought, when I entered, it was a Catholic cathedral." "No," he said, "it is a Protestant." We engaged in conversation along a religious line, and exchanged our views in such a way that neither took offense. Went by train to the celebrated Blarney Castle, a distance of five miles, and paid a sixpence at the entrance of the park. The Castle is of stone, with a tower 120 feet high, and was built by Comac McCarthy in the fifteenth century. The attendant, who is an old lady, said to me: "Don't be comin' down without yez kiss the Blarney stone." I climbed up the old stone stairway, and on reaching the top inquired of a young man where the famous stone was. He kindly pointed it out to me; it was on a projecting buttress between two iron bars. There is a battlement around the top of the castle, and in order to kiss the stone it is necessary to be held by the heels while you perform this wonderful feat. When he informed me how it was reached, my desire was not strong enough to take the risk of being gathered up from below in a condition to be laid away in some cemetery in Old Ireland. I heard a secretary from England relating his experience of being held by the feet while he gave the stone his compliments. Once was sufficient for him, he said. When I came down, the old lady said: "Did you kiss the Blarney stone?" "No," I replied, "I will save my kisses until I get back to America. I'll not waste them on a stone." The park, in which the castle stands, is nicely shaded, and is used as a quiet little picnic resort. There were several private parties there then, who seemed to be having a pleasant time. I remained there a short time and wrote up my diary for the day. Spent the evening in the Y. M. C. A. hall with a Mr. McC——, who gave me considerable information about the city. William Penn, founder of Pennsylvania, was converted to Quakerism in the city of Cork.

FRIDAY, July 20.—Left the city of Cork at 10:30 A. M. for the city of Limerick. At the station a mother seemed very much distressed, for her daughter, a young lady of about eighteen years, was leaving home for a distant city. As the train moved off, leaving the mother on the platform, the daughter, who was in the compartment I was in, burst into a flood of tears. I remarked to her, "It is rather hard, parting with friends." "Oh, yes," she replied, "I am leaving home for the first time." But the tears were soon brushed away, for when the train moved slowly into the station at Limerick, I noticed a tall, handsome young man walking along and looking very anxiously into the different compartments, and when their eyes met, the sunshine came into both of their faces. It might have been her big brother, but I thought there was too much sentiment for a tie of that sort. The country from Cork to Limerick is quite as fine as in any part of Ireland. I noticed a great many thrifty looking farms, and I should judge the soil was very fertile. Limerick has a population of 40,000. I have heard a great deal about the city, for I have an old friend who lived there when young. Some of the buildings had the appearance of being very ancient. There were some very pretty parts which I passed through. As I had only a few hours to remain there, I kept on the move. I passed down the principal thoroughfare, on which were a number of attractive looking stores, then over one of the bridges spanning the river Shannon, into a section where there were a number of little, forlorn looking shanties. There are several nice churches in this city, which is something that graces any city or town. I called on Rev. Mr. A——, pastor of the Wesleyan Church. He had just been appointed there, his last charge being in Belfast. He and his wife welcomed me to their home, and made my short stay in Limerick a very pleasant one. In bidding them good bye, I felt I was able to add two more choice friends of the good old Irish type to my already lengthy list. A journey of a few miles brought me to the town of Tipperary, where I called on Mr. H——, father of one of the gentlemen I met at Londonderry. He keeps a large drapery (or dry goods store, as we would style it), and has quite a number of clerks in his employ, most of whom board with him, that being the custom in that country. He insisted on my remaining with him over night. He and his son, a young man, comprise his immediate family, his wife being deceased. His housekeeper was a very agreeable lady, and spared no pains to make my visit pleasant. She was a devout Roman Catholic, as were all the clerks. Mr. H—— is a Methodist, the only one in the town, but I was informed he had the respect of the entire community, irrespective of creed. After tea Mr. H—— showed me through the town. It contains a large Catholic church, a Presbyterian church, and Church of Ireland; there are three banks, and several stores of fair size. We went to New Tipperary, which is at the extreme end of the old town, and built within a few years past. We passed a number of little cabins in going there, and as I looked into the open doors I wondered how people managed to live in such a small place, especially some of the families, who seemed to have a good supply of children. We stood on the top of Mutton Pie Hill, and from its peak had a good view of the country and town. It rained nearly every day I was in Ireland, so while up on this hill, which bears such a suggestive name (especially to a hungry man), down came the usual shower-bath, and compelled us to hurriedly seek shelter.

SATURDAY, July 21.—Mr. H—— accompanied me to the railroad station, and while waiting for the train we gathered some shamrock. Left Tipperary on the 8 A. M. train for Dublin; passed through Goold's Cross, Cashnell, Templemore, Ballybrophy and one or two more towns, which, a gentleman sitting next to me informed me, were in County Tipperary; Mount Rath, Marysborough, Port Arlington, in Queen's County. In Kildair, saw the cavalrymen drilling on a splendid drill-ground. We arrived in Dublin at 11:45 A. M. Secretary B—— gladdened my heart by presenting me some mail matter from *home*. Mr. S—— invited me to spend the evening with him at Kingstown, and as the yachts Vigilant and Brittania were to race there in the afternoon, Secretary B—— requested me to go with him to witness the race. It was a gala day at Kingstown harbor, and an immense crowd were gathered there. We walked out on the long pier and saw the boats coming in the distance, the Vigilant on the lead, and while on the pier, met Mr. F——, and we went to Mr. B——'s and sat by the window and saw the boats pass that were causing so much excitement on both sides of the Atlantic. Mr. B—— said to me, "of course you are rejoicing to see the Vigilant coming in ahead." "Well," I replied, "I have been claimed as a native of the "Old Sod" so much I can scarcely tell which one I am interested in." In the evening Mr. S—— and myself went to Victoria Mountain and Killiney Hill, which overlooks Kingstown, and from which can be seen the town of Bray, in County Wicklow. We remained until it began to grow dark, and the lights at Bray and Kingstown were a fine sight.

SUNDAY, July 22.—Went to the Centenary Wesleyan Chapel, at Stephen's Green. The Rev. Wesley G——, the pastor, preached a grand sermon. From where I sat he had the appearance of a comparatively young man. In a conversation with a Rev. Mr. B—— the next day, I remarked that Rev. Mr. G—— was a rising young preacher. He laughed and said, "he is as old as I am," and he was a man well advanced in life. He remarked that several had been mistaken like myself, seeing him at a distance. In the afternoon, attended the Sabbath school of the Lower Abbey Street Wesleyan Chapel. The superintendent requested me to teach a class of young lads, and after teaching the lesson, I gave them an account of Sunday school work in America. They were very much interested. I did not think any one knew me, and was much surprised when the pastor came to me and requested me to sing "A Sinner Like Me," as he understood I had written it. A young man, whose name was W—— P——, came to me at the close and said: "I told the pastor about you; I met you at the Hall." Went to the service at this old church in the evening, and heard the newly appointed pastor preach on, "It is a Faithful Saying," etc. At 9 P. M., found a large gathering at the Y. M. C. A. hall, and did what I could to advance the Master's Kingdom there. So closed my second Sabbath in Dublin.

MONDAY, July 23.—Left Harcourt Street Station at 9:30 for Fox Rock, a suburb six miles from Dublin, containing many splendid homes with well arranged grounds. Relatives of particular friends of mine in America live there. I called at their fine home, expecting to remain there only a short time, then take the train for Bray, in County Wicklow, but while in conversation with Miss G——, her mother ordered the groom to harness the horse to the jaunting car, and, when she came into the parlor, said she had planned a drive for us to County Wicklow, and intended returning by way of Bray. I had learned considerable of the hospitality of that country, and accepted the invitation. Just as Miss G—— and her mother and I were about leaving the house for the drive, the Rev. Mr. B——, a fine old gentleman, pastor of a church on the suburbs of Dublin, called, and Mrs. G—— invited him to accompany us. As we rode down through the Scalp, the large rocks, which were piled up on each side like a huge wall, looked as though they had fallen from the side of the mountain and the road had been cut through them. The roads all through the British Isles are well made and exceedingly level, so that one enjoys a ride over them very much. We stopped at Lord Powerscourt's domain, in County Wicklow. The scenery is very romantic. Between the mountains is a broad ravine with a beautiful stream of water hurrying down the rocks and finding its way out into the sea. Miss G—— drove around to the entrance at the other end of this large and grand domain, and we walked leisurely through it, and I enjoyed every moment I spent there. We met an old man with a violin, sitting on a rock. Mrs. G—— requested him to play one of their popular airs. He brought the music out of his instrument in a way that indicated he had been using the bow for many years. As we stood on a ledge of rocks and looked down into the ravine below, I wished for a kodak, that I might get the picture to carry back to America. Rev. B—— was quite a poet, and read us some of his latest poems. We passed through the grounds and joined Miss G—— again, and drove down through Bray, which is a pleasant town on the coast. On our way homeward we passed through a little town, and saw two small children, one of whom was entirely blind; they began begging for pennies, and we threw them some; this encouraged them to continue their asking, and the girl grasped the hand of the blind boy and ran down the road after us for quite a distance. I was informed that Ireland was a land of beggars, but I saw comparatively few of them. At least there were not many that annoyed me; they may have had an idea that my funds were low. When we returned to the house, a dinner that would do credit to any home awaited us, which I most thoroughly enjoyed. Rev. Mr. B—— and I returned to Dublin and I took a walk along the Quay, past the Four Courts, and saw St. Patrick's Cathedral in the distance. It is said to be built on the spot where St. Patrick built a church, and near a well where he baptized his converts. I bade good bye to many of those whom I have every reason to call genuine friends, and began making preparations to leave the Emerald Isle, for which I shall always have a good warm feeling. Mr. W—— P—— invited me to spend the evening with him at his home. He is a young man in whom I was deeply interested, and, if the way is opened for him, will make a useful man to the Wesleyan Church, of which he is a member. When I bade Secretary B—— good bye, I said to him: "If ever I should have the pleasure of meeting you or any of my friends from this side of the Atlantic in America, I will use the same club of kindness that you have beaten me with. A few months ago he came over to attend the Y. M. C. A. Convention at Springfield, Mass., and at its close spent a few days with me, and I did my best to square accounts with him. His discourse at Tabernacle M. E. Church, Camden, N. J., on Sunday, and the ones at Bethany M. E. Church and at the Y. M. C. A. hall, in the afternoon, gave the people who heard him an idea of the kind of lads that grow in Ireland.

Tuesday, July 24.—Left the old city of Dublin from North Wall for Holyhead, Wales, and ran into a storm before getting out of the river Liffey, and, upon reaching the mouth of the river, saw that the Irish Sea was bent on having a row with our steamer. We had not gotten far beyond the point called Ireland's Eye before the angry waves began to dash over us. It seemed to be the day for settling up accounts, for nearly every one was busy. Among the passengers were a number of soldiers, going home on furloughs; they may have been very valiant on land, but the old Irish Sea was a "wee bit" too much for them, and from the appearance of some, she nearly used them up. Where was Butler? some one might ask. Well, he was busy ciphering with the rest, and sighing for a quiet harbor. In a letter I wrote to Mr. B—— after returning to England, told him I had formed a strong attachment for Ireland and many of her sons and daughters, but had no love for the Irish sea, for no sooner was I in her grasp than she robbed me of my morning meal, and tussled with me for the previous one. That ride of a few hours on the belligerent Irish Sea was more uncomfortable than my trip across the Atlantic. The chopped sea is trying to a ship, but more so to a person not accustomed to that kind of treatment. We took the train at Holyhead, and was soon hurrying along through the romantic country of North Wales. Would like very much to have spent some time there, for the mountain scenery was charming. On the steamer I became quite well acquainted with a Mr. L——, of Westport, County Mayo, Ireland, and we rode together on the train as far as Bangor. The tubular bridge, in Wales, interested me. Passed through a great many pretty towns in Wales and England. Wolverhampton is a large manufacturing town in England. Arrived at Harborn at 9 P. M., and enjoyed another pleasant evening at "my English home."

Back Again to Old England.

WEDNESDAY, July 25.—Went to the Wesleyan Church at St. Martin's and Islington road, the seat of the British Conference. The admission was by ticket. One of the ministers interested himself in trying to get me a ticket, but the demand had been so great that he failed, so I went back to Harborn. The public schools had their annual celebration on the cricket fields near Mr. P——'s home, and the field sports, running matches, and the excellent drill given by the lancers, pleased the large concourse of people greatly. I availed myself of an opportunity of giving a temperance lecture to a young man from London, whom I met on the grounds, but he failed to see the danger of strong drink, which has been the overthrow of so many. The fireworks in the evening were magnificent, especially the last piece, entitled, "Thanks to All."

THURSDAY, July 26.—The Sabbath school of the old Harborn Church and the day school joined in a celebration and parade; they made a nice display, passing through the streets. I assisted in trimming the national school-room, where the children were lunched. In the afternoon they finished the day on the field adjoining the rector's residence, some of the young people—and a sprinkling of the older ones, too—joining in the merry dance. The brass band played some airs that made the dancers bound quite lively. As I watched the children and older people enjoying themselves with various games, I concluded that English people get out of a picnic all there is in it.

FRIDAY, July 27.—Mr. P—— and I went to the steamship office in Birmingham, where I engaged my berth on the steamer "Southwark," sailing for Philadelphia on August 22d; from there we went by tram to Handsworth, a part of Birmingham, and went through the old Handsworth church. Like all the old churches, there were old tablets and marble slabs with the names of some who lived far back in the past. There was a short service held while we were there; the congregation was very small, consisting of four ladies, Mr. P——, and myself. Mr. P—— said the rector read the service at that hour, whether there was any one there or not. On my return to Harborn, stopped at the seat of the British Conference. Went into the chapel-yard just in time to assist in caring for a little boy, a son of one of the ministers, who had suddenly fallen in a fainting fit, and was thought by his anxious father and mother to be dying, but after some remedies were applied by a physician, he recovered sufficiently to be removed to their home in a carriage. In the evening I was invited to the home of W—— C——'s head gardener, and with the good natured, jolly Englishman and his family, spent the evening very pleasantly.

SATURDAY, July 28.—Left Birmingham by the Great Western Railroad for Stratford-on-Avon, and arrived there at 11 A. M. Called on the secretary of the little Y. M. C. A., and after a short talk with him, he accompanied me to the old church where Shakespeare and his wife are buried. I admired the quiet old town as I passed through its wide, clean looking streets on my way to this historic church. The grave of Shakespeare is inside the chancel rail, a plain flagstone marking the spot. On the chancel wall is a bust of the great poet. There was an old Bible with the record of his baptism. The churchyard which overlooks the beautiful river Avon, contains a great many very old tombstones. Leaving there, we walked over to Ann Hathaway's cottage, in the little village of Shottery. It was a beautiful walk of about one mile through the meadows. I came to an old thatched roof cottage, and thought it looked ancient enough for the Hathaway cottage, but found I was mistaken and was directed to it by a policeman. I went to the door and was met by a small girl, who informed me the admittance fee was a sixpence. On entering this, the quaintest house I was ever in, I met an old lady, the attendant, Mrs. B—— by name, who informed me she was a descendent of Ann Hathaway, and began showing me some of the old relics. In the old chimney corner was a ham closet which she said was used in Ann Hathaway's time, and an old oaken bench that she was very particular in telling me Shakespeare and Ann were supposed to have sat on when courting. I said to her: "Let me sit on it; I may get an inspiration," but she kept on with her description of the various old pieces of furniture without paying much attention to my request. She showed me an old table and some chinaware that belonged to Ann. A lady and gentleman came in while she was showing me through, and while she was repeating the old, old story to them, I wrote in my note book, sitting by the table referred to. She said to us: "There is an old bedstead upstairs that I will show you; it belonged to Ann Hathaway, and is 400 years old." So we followed the old lady (who informed us she was eighty years of age) to the room above. She gave us the history of this old bedstead, which looked solid enough to stand as many more years. As I was looking at the walls, which were completely covered with names, she said: "Oliver Wendell Holmes wrote his name on these walls when here on a visit, but it is against the rules to write on them now." I replied: "It is because there is no more room, if that is the rule." I am not given to putting my name in public places, but concluded that if possible my name should be among those on these walls. Near the window I saw a space and hurriedly wrote my name while she was engaged in conversation with the lady and gentleman, but just as I was finishing, she looked up and said: "Oh, don't do that," and repeated, "it's against the rule." I do not often break the rules of any place I visit, but the temptation was too strong to resist. When I was leaving the cottage she said to me, "You can pick some leaves from that bush near the old well, which I did, and pressed them in my guide book, and also drank from the old well. The lady informed me she had lived in the cottage for seventy years. From there I walked back to Stratford with the gentleman and his wife, who were from Worcester. I was surprised when they informed me they had never visited Ann Hathaway's cottage before, although living only a few miles from it. Then I visited Shakespeare's old home. The first floor is a museum containing relics which belonged to this noted man : among them was a sword, and a letter written by Mr. Richard Quyney to Shakespeare in 1589, and some early editions of some of his first plays. I wrote my name in the visitors' book, where I noticed the names of a great many Americans. From the museum, I climbed the quaint old stairway and went into the room where, nearly three hundred years ago, this wonderful character made his advent into this great world. It is said this room is in its original state, except that persons from various parts of the world have written their names on the walls until there does not appear to be space enough to write another. It is said Byron, Scott, Washington Irving, George IV.—the Prince of Orange—the Duke of Wellington, Tom Moore, and Dickens are among the noted men who have inscribed their names on the walls. I was shown into a very small room, which one of the attendants told me was used by Shakespeare's father as a wool-room. The Shakespeare Memorial, a monument erected by the late George W. Childs, of Philadelphia, is quite an ornament to the beautiful town of Stratford. As I sat on a bench in the old churchyard on the banks of the river Avon, I saw in the distance the handsome Shakespeare Memorial Theatre. As I left this interesting old town, I thought the day spent there would long to be remembered. I have already referred to my expected visit to Worcestershire. I had purposed spending a month in and around South Littleton, and had engaged my boarding place, but spent more time in other parts than I intended, so could only stay in this locality for a few days. It is a ride of about fourteen miles from Stratford-on-Avon to South Littleton. I had written to Mr. B——, a relative of my old friend, Mr. R——, of Camden, New Jersey, that I would be there on Saturday afternoon, and when I left the train expected to find him at the station, but saw no one that I thought answered his description. Upon inquiring of the station master, he, pointing to a young man sitting in a cart a little beyond the station, said : "there is his son, waiting for you." There was a huge smile that took possession of his face when he saw me approaching the cart. He seemed greatly pleased to see me, and gave me a look that seemed to say, "if you are a sample, they must raise some tall lads in America." I seated myself beside him ; he applied the home-made whip to the animal, and I was soon bouncing along toward the little town, whose church spire I could see about a mile distant. We rode through the quiet, old-fashioned town, passing down a little street just beside the old church. As we drove up to the house, which is more than 200 years old, the mother and the other two sons came out, and any one would have thought, by the warm welcome I received, that I was a relative coming home. When I came to the door, found it necessary for me to bend considerably in order to avoid a collision with the top. The floors were of stone, laid, I judge, in whatever manner the builder of long-ago happened to gather hold of them. There were the old open fire-place, with a tea kettle hanging from a long hook, boiling away for my benefit, and seats in the chimney corner, upon which I frequently sat and sang, accompanied by my autoharp. Mr. B——, who was obliged to go to Evesham, a town a few miles away, on business, came home shortly after my arrival, and as we gathered around the family board and partook of the palatable meal prepared by the good lady, Mrs. B——, and talked of the friends in far-away America, I had the same homelike feeling that took possession of me when visiting a great number of homes through the British Isles. Board had been engaged for me at the home of Mr. M——, the village blacksmith, in another part of the town. While on our way there, in passing the churchyard, they pointed out a freshly made grave and said to me: "They buried the remains of a young man there this afternoon, who, while on a drunken debauch, blew his brains out. He left a wife, two small children and a widowed mother. I met them a few days afterward, coming from the graveyard, and I thought as I saw that sorrow stricken young widow, and the mother, who was being supported by the hands of kind friends, as they led her back to their desolate home, surely every Christian, as well as good-inclined people ought to be engaged in trying to crush out the great "Demon Rum." The house in which Mr. M—— lived was a large, comfortable one, but quite as old as the one I had just left. The old stone floors, and chimney corner, and old-fashioned windows, with their broad casements, which could be used as a seat very nicely, and in which I sat and wrote to the friends at home, struck me as being very quaint. The family at home consisted of Mrs.

M—— and her daughter, a young lady who showed the excellent trait of being kind and attentive to her mother. Mr. M—— was away on business; the other four members of the family, with the exception of a very bright, intelligent girl of about fourteen, who was living at Evesham, were married and live some distance away. I was soon made to feel at home, and in the few days I spent there, everything was done to make my stay a pleasant one. Mrs. M—— said to me: "Mr. Butler, I never saw an American before; you seem very much like our own people," and I am sure I felt as though after such pleasant associations with the people during my sojourn in the British Isles, that they were "bone of my bone and flesh of my flesh."

SUNDAY, July 29.—There is an organization of about twenty persons who meet in a small hall for worship. Mr. B—— is a member; he came to the house and invited me to go with him to the men's Bible class, which meets in the morning. I found them earnestly engaged in studying the Bible, and was quite interested in listening to old and young giving very intelligent answers to the questions being asked. There is a chain of little towns in this rural district— South Littleton, Middle Littleton, North Littleton, Badesy and several others in a radius of a few miles—and this Bible class was made up of men from these towns. In the afternoon, visited a man living near by who had been helpless with rheumatism for nine years, and in the meantime had had several hemorrhages. He had one of the most interesting faces I ever looked into, and was a man of considerable intelligence and possessed Christian resignation. I frequently went into his humble little home and sang for him. He would often request me to play and sing, "In That City," and say to me, as a smile would play over his face, "I expect to soon be there," and, like my old Scotch friend that I visited at Sterling, he has since gone to live in that "Heavenly City." In the evening the hall was crowded with an attentive congregation. At the close of the service I was requested to give them an entertainment some evening during the week. I informed them I had never been the central figure in an entertainment, but would do my best.

MONDAY, July 30.—Mr. W—— B—— and I went through the old church—the original one built nine hundred years ago—and through the yard, which contains many old tombs, some of which date back as far as 1690. Some of the readers may think I have a weakness for wandering through old graveyards, and I confess, whenever I passed an old church or churchyard, I felt inclined to halt and read the quaint old epitaphs. Mr. B—— and I walked to Bidford, a town four miles distant, and in going there passed through some of the towns I have already mentioned. Bidford is a neat, pretty little town situated along the river Avon, which flows through this beautiful country. This was the old home of Mrs. R——, wife of my friend, Mr. R——, and she desired me to inquire after her relatives, whom she had not heard from for years. Mr. B—— introduced me to an old man who, when I inquired about the relatives of this lady, said to me: "I know them very well, and I remember her fifty years ago." He directed us to where one of her brothers was at work on a farm on the outskirts of the town. We inquired for him of some women who were picking berries. One of them said: "You are from America." "Yes," I replied. "Well, I have an old aunt living with a Mr. L——, in St. Louis," she further remarked. "That is several hundred miles from where I live," I said. One of the women said: "I am the wife of the nephew of Mrs. R—— and will call Mr. B——, my uncle." When the old man came to where we were, and I told him that I was requested to call on him, by his sister in America, he was quite broken up, and said: "I thought she was dead years ago. And is my sister living?" It surely was good news from a faraway country to that old man. In the evening, quite a number of the young people met at Mr. B——'s, and I sat in the old seat in the chimney corner and entertained them with several harp solos and a description of the wonderful country from whence I came.

TUESDAY, July 31.—Sat in the old window case and wrote a long descriptive letter to my uncle, who had written to me expressing himself as desirous of being with me, to rummage through the old ruins of England. In this old town, nearly every house gave evidence of having been built when our country was in its infancy. Most of the day was spent in practicing for the coming entertainment. Miss M—— was an excellent violinist, and Mr. F—— B—— understood how to get the sweet strains from this instrument also, and a Mr. J——, of Birmingham, who was visiting in the village, could use his voice in song quite well, so I began making up a fair program. After a delightful walk to the new home which Mr.

B—— was building, I returned and spent the evening at Mrs. M——'s, with a number of friends who were interested in the concert, which was being advertised in the villages. It was looked forward to as being one of the greatest events in years, and I thought it would be when I appeared on the stage.

WEDNESDAY, August 1.—Went by train to the town of Evesham, about four miles away. I did not think to find it such a large and interesting place. Its ancient looking houses and buildings so attracted me that I spent nearly the whole day there. I passed through a very narrow street to two old churches which stand near each other, surrounded by a large old churchyard. They were built near the line of two parishes, divided by an old bell tower built in 1520. Near the Roman Arch is an old house, which, an old man informed me, was the only original one in the town. In making some purchases at one of the stores, I had a long conversation with the proprietor and another gentleman, and found they, like most people of that country, were quite willing to listen to an account of America. The river Avon divides the town, and some of the residences have beautiful lawns sloping to the edge of the river. Near the bridge which spanned the river at one of the main streets, I saw a sign on a public house, as they style them over there, bearing the name of "The Angel Inn." I thought surely that is not an appropriate name for a place of that kind, but afterward concluded it was, for I remembered there were two kinds of angels. I remained in this interesting old town until late in the afternoon, and think I saw it pretty thoroughly.

This was the evening of the grand vocal and instrumental concert, and long before the time for the commencement, the village lasses had donned their best gowns, and with the lads of their choice were making their way to the hall. When the talent arrived we had great difficulty in getting to the platform, for young and old had packed the little hall. The concert began at the appointed time, with Butler the most conspicuous of all the talent (for they were all of small stature), master of ceremonies. We had been very economical in getting up our programs. I think we had but two, and they were not very elaborate; only a plain piece of paper with the order of exercises written with lead pencil. Miss M—— and Mr. B—— gave some very good violin solos, and Mr. J—— sang some pieces which called forth heavy encores. I was sandwiched in with an autoharp solo, and was requested to sing and play, "Old Folks at Home," and then give them a short address on the colored race. Very few had ever seen a Negro. "God Save the Queen" was the closing piece. Well, our homespun concert, gotten up by Butler, the amateur professor, was appreciated by the entire audience. The proceeds were for the organ fund.

THURSDAY, August 2.—I had a very pressing invitation to go with a number of persons from the different towns, on a picnic to the town of Broadway, seven miles distant, standing on a high hill. They told me it was the oldest town in that vicinity, and were anxious that I should see it, but my days in England were numbered, and it was necessary for me to pack my bundle and be on the move. I made the acquaintance of some excellent people in this as well as in the adjoining villages. I was interested in getting the young men organized into a society of some kind, which would fit them for greater usefulness, and talked to a number of them about it, and promised, when I returned to London, to get some plans in printed form from the secretary of the Y. M. C. A. at Exeter Hall. Left on the 5 P. M. train for Birmingham, arriving at Harborn in time to spend the evening with the kind friends there.

FRIDAY, August 3.—Mr. E—— P—— and I went to Birmingham and called at Cook's office and made inquiry concerning a trip to Antwerp, Belgium, then sallied forth to see more of this fine old city. Some of its streets had become quite familiar to me. We were invited to the home of a Mr. D——, a druggist by whom Mr. E—— P—— was formerly employed, and I spent a few hours very pleasantly in another good old English home. Another budget of mail awaited me when I returned to Harborn. It seemed strange as I read of the extreme heat in America--the thermometer crowding beyond 100°—for I had been using my overcoat and heavy clothing most of the summer. It was moderately warm through the day, but in the evening, as a rule, it was cool enough for a "top coat." I enjoyed a long walk through the town of Harborn, and returning, stood on the hill near the church, where I had a view of the country for miles around.

SATURDAY, August 4.—Purchased my ticket at Cook's office for Antwerp, and left on the 11:20 A. M. express for London. It was the Saturday prior to

Bank Holiday, and the trains were greatly crowded. Hundreds of people were leaving the city for points all along the road. We changed cars at Leicester, a town of considerable size, having the appearance of being a beautiful place. I left by the through line, and as there were comparatively few going from this point to London, most of the passengers taking the train I would have taken but for a slight misunderstanding, I rode all the way, the sole occupant of the compartment. In traveling in England, one has to look out for himself generally. The guards, as a rule, are gentlemanly, but are not so particular in informing you of the changes as they might be. I arrived there at 3:30 P. M. and went to my old quarters on Bernard street, and then called on Mr. H—— S——, and then took the long ride to Stamford Hill and spent another enjoyable evening at "Hope Lodge," with Friend S—— and family.

SUNDAY, August 5.—I was pleased to be able to spend another Sunday in London. When I went to the Great Queen Street Church, it seemed something like going back home. The friends gave me a hearty welcome. On my way home I stopped at the Lincoln-on-Field Church, and then went to Liverpool road to inquire after a friend, and in coming back came down the St. Pancras road, where I met a number of Salvationists and engaged in conversation with some of them. All over that great city these men and women can be seen pushing forward the cause of their dear Master. When I returned to the house for dinner, I met another native of Calcutta, who was in London studying medicine, and expected to graduate the following week. In the evening, as I was going into church with friend H—— S——, Mr. A——, a local preacher, accosted me and requested me to go with him to Parker street, West Centre, to the county council lodging, where he was to conduct a service. It is a place nicely fitted up as a cheap lodging place for men who were out of employment. The service was held in the reading-room, which is quite large. There were about one hundred and fifty men, old and young, assembled; most of them were smoking and reading. Mr. A—— said they usually did not pay much attention. Two young ladies accompanied us; one presided at the piano, and the other sang a solo. As she sang a beautiful and touching piece, they were very attentive. Then Mr. A—— introduced me to the audience and announced I would sing, accompanied by my harp. After I had played and sang a piece for them, several exclaimed: "Much obliged to you." It rather surprised me to be applauded in that style. After the service many of them gathered about me and shook my hand, and said: "God bless you, and give you a safe passage across the Atlantic." I returned to Great Queen Street Church to the Communion service, which was conducted a little different from the way they are in America.

MONDAY, August 6.—This was Bank Holiday, and business, as a rule, was suspended, and it seemed that all that could were making their way to the parks and pleasure resorts in and around the city, about which could be seen the large posters giving notice of some grand Bank Holiday excursion. I expected to leave by train in the evening for Harwich, and from there by steamer for Antwerp. Went to Cook's tourist office at Ludgate Circus and got some English money exchanged for Belgium, and then took a stroll through Cheapside, noted for its handsome stores. From this great thoroughfare ran a number of small streets that have quite a history. Bread street, which is quite small, is where Milton, the great poet, was born. Milk street, also bearing a suggestive name, is where Sir Thomas Moore was born, and on it stood Mermaid Inn, a favorite place of Shakespeare. Fleet street, running from St. Paul's to the Strand, has an interesting history to all lovers of Dickens' works, for on this street stood the Fleet Prison, made famous by him. It seemed to me that you could not go anywhere but you were informed that some great man was born there, or some important event happened there, and as I walked through the streets of London I felt very desirous of spending several weeks more in sightseeing. The Mansion House, the palace of the Lord Mayor, is a splendid building, as is also the Royal Exchange. The carvings upon it are magnificent. I remained here some time in looking at this fine building. In the afternoon I went out again to what Mr. S—— and family styled my "London Home," at Stamford Hill. Mr. S——and his youngest son and I went to the beautiful Finsbury Park, and I should judge from the immense throng of people who were enjoying themselves there, it was a place very much appreciated by the residents of that part of the city. It was laid out very nicely; the great beds of flowers were arranged in the most artistic manner, and there was a miniature lake on which were a number of small boats, well patronized. At 8 P. M., boarded the train for Harwich. In the compartment were three young men, who, like myself, were not hard to become acquainted with. One of them was a jolly lad, and by his witty remarks amused his little audience. They were speaking of the towns they came from, and I asked this bundle of fun what part of England he thought I was from. He replied: "I guess you are from America." He had heard me use the word guess, common to Americans. We left Harwich for Antwerp at 9:30, and I soon retired.

In Holland and Belgium.

TUESDAY, August 7.—Arose about 4 A. M., and when I came on deck we were in sight of Holland. We met a great many odd looking fishing boats. Their dark looking sails and tub-like shape attracted my attention. I met the three gentlemen again on deck, and the clown, as I styled him, saw the funny side of everything, and had a way of making us see it. I shall not soon forget that chap who made the trip to Antwerp so pleasant for me. We stopped just off Flushing, Holland, and took on the pilot. We were near enough to the city to see that it was a place of some note. There was a Catholic priest on board with whom I became acquainted. He informed me he was stationed near the town of Leeds, England, but his home was in Antwerp. He said he had a strong desire to go to America, but when he mentioned it to his old widowed mother, it grieved her very much, and he could not withstand her tears. He seemed to possess a fine Christian spirit. As we came in sight of Antwerp, he pointed out the places of interest. It is a great shipping place, and the masts of the ships seemed to be lifting their heads in all directions. Our bundle of fun was disappointed in not having his friend meet him at the wharf, and walked with the other two men and myself to the street running along the river front. He would stop and call the attention of the passersby to the address of the place he expected to go, but no one that we met understood English. We soon had a crowd of men and boys following us, all anxious to understand enough to pilot him to his destination. This amused me very much, as the people came to the store doors and watched us. Finally he found a man who spoke English, as also the other two did, and so we separated, they going to the hotel with their guide, and I to the Exhibition. A sense of loneliness came over me as I realized I was alone in a land where I, as a rule, could not be understood. The Exhibition was a repetition of what I had seen in America, but I would have been very much interested had I had some one with me. For once in my life I had come to a place where I found it impossible to converse with any one. The great crowds of people I passed where talking in an unknown tongue. I saw a very striking figure of Christ on the cross, in life size, with two figures each side of him. A large harp made of artificial flowers attracted the attention of many people. The American exhibits were not very elaborate. The Midway Plaisance and the Zulu Village, with a number of natives rowing on a miniature lake, singing some hideous song, seemed to draw most of the crowd. The furniture, tapestry and statuary in the main building, and the machinery hall claimed my attention for some time. I spent most of the day there without saying very much to anyone. Just before I left I became acquainted with a gentleman from Belfast, Ireland, and I assure you was glad to find some one that I could converse with. He went to London on the steamer, and invited me go to the wharf with him—which I did. I felt inclined to shake off the dust of the city and return to England also, but I wanted to pay a visit to Brussels and purposed spending the night and the following day there. When I boarded the street car, I said to the conductor: "I want to go to Brussels Station." He shrugged his shoulders, shook his head and gave me a look that indicated he would like to help me out. I began to appreciate the feelings of people who came to our shores without a knowledge of our language. "Can you tell me how I will reach the Brussels Station," I repeated. Finally by motions and spreading my hands in a great manner, much to the amusement of the passengers, made him understand where I wanted to go, and on reaching the boulevard leading to the depot, he motioned for me to get off the car. As I made my way to the station, concluded not to take a trip to a country again without knowing something of the language or having company. Many of the streets of Antwerp are very beautiful and are kept in excellent order; as I passed along the boulevard leading to the station, noticed a great many fine houses. When I went to the office to get my ticket, just in front of me was a young man who greatly surprised me when he asked for six tickets for Brussels. I laid my hand on his shoulder and said to him: "Excuse me, sir, but I am so glad to hear a man speak English; are you going to Brussels?"

He gave me a look and seemed to take in the situation at once, and sympathizing with me in my lonely condition, said: "Yes; buy your ticket for the express and go along with us; there are three ladies and two other gentlemen in our party." I needed no further invitation for I felt I had suddenly fallen into the hands of a friend, and when we came to the platform I found three very refined looking ladies, and two gentlemen, whom anyone at a glance would have known were excellent people. They were from Bradford, England. The young man said to them by way of an introduction: "This is another American gentleman who is going to Brussels with us," and turning to me, remarked: "We met a gentleman from your country who will join us in a short time." We had the compartment to ourselves; the partitions being low, the people in the ajoining one seemed very much interested in our English conversation. The American finally put in an appearance and became very friendly with me. "If you have no objection," I said to the Englishman, "I would like to stop at the same hotel with you." He kindly said: "You are entirely welcome to go with us." On reaching the hotel, the maid showed us to our rooms and I was well pleased with my quarters; but presently she came up stairs and said in broken English to the American and I: "These rooms are engaged by those other people and we have no vacant rooms, but the proprietor has gone to another hotel below here to get you accommodations." This young woman was the only one about the house who made any attempt to speak English, and she knew very little more about it than I did about French, which as a rule, is spoken in Belgium. Presently the information came to us that rooms had been secured for us, so we followed the young man, the proprietor, to a very genteel looking place and no one in this house could speak a word of English. The lady showed us to our apartments, and as there were no matches in the room, I asked her for some. She smiled, and shrugged her shoulders, as is their custom when they do not understand. I saw at once that I would have to use my hands instead of my tongue, so began to make motions on the wall and point to the gas. She seemed to enjoy it for she went out laughing and soon returned with the needed article. The American invited me to go out with him, but concluded to retire and be prepared for the tramp I had planned for the following day. During the night I was awakened by some one trying my door and thought now I will have to prepare to defend my pocket-book, but on investigation found it was the American. He called to me and said: "Do you know your key is on the outside of the door?" "No," I replied, I thought I locked my door on retiring. He considered me very careless, which was the case, and I then made sure the key was in its proper place.

WEDNESDAY, August 8.—Before any of the friends whom I met the day previous, were on the scene of action, I was on the streets of the magnificent city of Brussels, inquiring my way to the places of interest, but met with very little success, in getting any information. The first place on my program was the Cathedral, and I thought as I stepped up to a priest on the street, I was sure of being directed there, but to my surprise, he began to elevate his shoulders and shake his head, and I was obliged to pass on; so concluded to try again. This time I showed another priest a cut of a cathedral at Ghent. He looked at it and then began pointing in a way that indicated to me he thought it was Ghent that I was inquiring about. I shook my head, and he gave me a look which seemed to say, I would help you if I could. Finally I caught sight of the tall spire and wended my way through the crooked streets to the grand old structure. There were many devout worshippers, but they did not seem to be disturbed as the visitors walked around. In one end of the Cathedral there was a pulpit that attracted my attention. It was supported by two carved figures representing stalwart men, with an angel each side of the stairway and a number of other designs on the pulpit, which were magnificent. Leaving there, I went to Hotel de Ville, which is a large, handsome structure, originally built 1402-43, and has a tall, stately spire 370 feet high, with a colossal statue of St. Michael on top. Saw a great number of carriages standing in front of the hotel, and quite a crowd about the entrance, so my curiosity caused me to halt. Presently, saw a wedding party coming out, which struck me as being a **grand affair**, judging from the ladies' gorgeous attire.

The bride's dress was of white silk, with material enough, apparently, for two ordinary costumes. A little maid followed in the rear holding fast to a part of it, keeping it clear from all incumbrances. This, being a bachelor's description, of course will not be considered as being entirely clear. Leaving this scene of gaiety, I went through the Arcade. It is a long arch, with beautiful stores on either side. Entering one of them, I made some purchases and was surprised when the young lady spoke to me in broken English. From there, went to a part of the city that contained many large and handsome edifices, which I judged were government and city buildings. I greatly admired the grand boulevards, which were lined on both sides with residences that would be ornamental to any city. The military parade interested me as it passed a nicely arranged park, at the entrance of which I was standing. There was a gentleman near me, whom I ventured to ask to direct me to the Antwerp Station. His shoulders began to take an upward course and his hands an outward turn, and it was evident that the information would not be forthcoming; but the thought occurred to me to try a little of the German language, and found, like myself, he understood something of it. It was sufficient to enable me to find my way to the station without much trouble. Having some time to spend before the train left for Antwerp, I went through what was, apparently, a very old part of the city, the houses being built principally of light stone. Waterloo is only a few miles distant, and I felt inclined to stop over another day and visit this historic old battlefield. I left this magnificent city, with its 475,000 inhabitants, well pleased with my visit there, although I had experienced so much difficulty in being understood. In the compartment I occupied returning to Antwerp, there was not one person who could understand a word of English, so I spent the time looking at the country as we passed along, and noted the different towns. There were a great many women at work in the fields, and in Antwerp I saw them on the wharves helping the men unload the boats. On arriving, finding I had considerable time for sightseeing, went through quite a number of the quaint old streets, and visited the Cathedral, which is said to be the finest in Belgium. It was built 1352-1530, and is 384 feet long and 130 feet high. A gentleman gave me a discription of this grand old Cathedral before taking my trip. I was very much disappointed in not being able to see the painting, "The Descent From the Cross," by Rubens, as it was veiled. It is said to be a masterpiece. The wooden shoes worn by the men who were cleaning the streets, were a novel thing to me. Antwerp is, apparently, a city that carries on considerable business with the outside world, for as I walked along the street on the river front, saw the flags flying from the ships, from different parts of the world. The population of Antwerp is 240,000. I left at 7:45 for Harwich on the steamer which was very much crowded; a number of the passengers had a weakness for the whiskey bottle, and with this disturbing article about, it was difficult for many of us to get much sleep.

In Old England Again.

THURSDAY, August 9.—When I came on deck the shores of old England greeted my eyes. Soon we ran into the quiet harbor and in a short time, were speeding away by train toward the busy city of London. The country we passed through, I found, like all the other parts of England which it was my pleasure to see, was greatly to be admired. We passed through a number of towns, some of which were beautiful; one in particular, the town of Colchester, I recollect it as being quite a large and pleasant looking place. We arrived in London at 8:30, affording me another day for sightseeing in the great metropolis. As I wended my way through its crowded streets and passed the vast number of large and attractive stores, well patronized, concluded after all there was not so much depression in business as one would imagine. In my travels through this wonderful city, as well as in other cities and towns on both sides of the Atlantic, I observed that the real cause of so much poverty and distress is, "Strong Drink." In the streets of this great city, I saw men and women, young and old, going into public houses, spending their shillings for intoxicating drink, when they had great need of going to the tailor for an outfit. In my tramping I came to a thoroughfare called Threadneedle Street, (a name very suggestive to a bachelor.) I was curious to learn the origin of such an odd name for a street, but had not time to look it up. Went through a part of the New Law Court, a large and attractive building, which is said to have cost $5,000,000. On my way down the Strand stopped at the old Church of St. Mary-le-Strand, where Thomas Becket was once priest. It bears the marks of years. I was also on Maiden Lane, where Voltair lived. Then went to Exeter Hall, a place that had become quite familiar to me. One is always sure of a cordial welcome there from the secretary or his worthy assistant, who gave me some printed forms and some instructions in reference to the Y. M. C. A. work, which I was to take to South Littleton, as I was anxious to have them organize an association there. A short distance from Exeter Hall is Convent Garden; it is a flower and vegetable market, and is said to be the chief market of the kind in London. Frequently in going to the Strand I would stop there and spend a little time in looking about. As my time was growing short in London, and this was my farewell visit, kept on the move. I had been to a number of the places referred to several times, yet learned something more of their history, and felt like paying another visit to them. Whitehall Palace was very interesting to me, and I would like to have seen more of it. It is said that this is the place where Henry VIII met Ann Boylen, and where he died. From there Elizabeth was taken to prison. Milton and Cromwell once lived there, and there the latter died. It is a large, massive old building. Also went to the famous Scotland Yards, the police headquarters, and it is an immense place.

The nephew of an old friend of mine in America, was on the police force, and he desired me to call and try to find out his whereabouts, but I did not succeed, as it would take to much of my time. I went to Stamford Hill to bid farewell to my friends at "Hope Lodge." When I grasped the hands of Mr. and Mrs. S——, and their three promising sons, and his mother, a woman of rare excellence, and bade them good-bye, I wished there was not such a wide stretch of water between England and America, so that I might have the pleasure of frequently visiting this home. But while I left these friends with a possibility of never seeing them again in this life, carried the remembrance of their kind deeds with me to America, and shall keep them in a good state of preservation throughout life. Rode on the tram to Holborn, then walked through Southampton Row and Russell Square to Bernard street, spending the evening with Mr. H—— S——, at Free Masons' Hall, and on returning home found one of the lodgers, a young man from the West Indies, in great trouble, having lost his pocket book with a large amount of money. He had my sympathy without my shillings, for I was keeping careful watch over them, wondering if I would be able to complete my plans without being stranded.

FRIDAY, August 10.—This being my last day in London, I was on the move very early. My first point was Peckham, where lived the brother of Mr. H——, of Camden, N. J., and whom I had not as yet seen, as he was out when I called. He had sent me an invitation to spend several days with him, which I was unable to do. I walked over the long-to-be-remembered Waterloo Bridge, and seated myself on the tram, and although I had been over the route several times, found many things to interest me in passing along. Telford road, on which Mr. H—— lived, is built up with fine homes on each side, and is a pleasant part of the city. The door bell was answered by Mr. H——, who met me as an old friend would another, and when I entered the parlor, was introduced to another brother from a distant town. As I intended leaving in the afternoon for Birmingham, my stay was brief; but while there, although not near time for the noonday meal, Mrs. H—— prepared dinner. They said: "We could not think of letting you leave London without taking a meal with us"—another demonstration of English hospitality. It did me good to see how delighted all those were to whom I took messages from friends in America. Leaving Peckham, I rode to Kings Cross, and from there returned to the house and soon bade farewell to the old city of London, and left St. Pancras Station for Birmingham, arriving there at 5:30. Just as I reached New street, the elements gave me a cordial reception, for the rain came down in torrents, compelling me to ride inside the bus, thus depriving me of my usual seat on top, which I so much enjoyed, in riding to Harborn.

SATURDAY, August 11.—Mr. E—— P—— and I went to Birmingham to Cook's office and left the order to call for my luggage, which was to be sent to the steamer Southwark at a given time. It began to seem as though my stay was rapidly drawing to a close, but aside from a desire to see friends in America, I wished to remain longer, for there were many places which I wished to visit, some of them full of interest to one who was fond of making a tour into the past. At 3 P. M., I boarded the train for South Littleton, arriving there at 6 P. M., and found the friends looking for the return of the wandering American. In the evening a few of the young men met at the home of Mr. M——. I was greatly amused while listening to them in their exceedingly broad manner of speaking, exchanging their views on different questions. One of them, a nephew of Mrs. M——, sat in the old chimney corner smoking his pipe, and frequently by his droll, witty remarks, would cause that little circle to laugh heartily—I laughed in a very high key and was generally the leading voice. In the company was a young man who had recently become a Christain through the efforts of this noble little band of young men; he had been rescued from a life of dissipation. He gave great promise of becoming a power for good.

SUNDAY, August 12.—Met the Bible Class at the hall. The lesson was from Luke ix, and it did me good, as those plain unassuming men brought up the precious truths from the unfathomable mines of God's word. They expressed themselves in a way that impressed me with the fact that they regarded the Bible as being the inspired word of God. In the evening some of the members of the Salvation Army from Evesham were present and took part in the service, at the close of which, about twenty persons assembled at the home of Mr. B——, and, as I sat in the chimney corner, and talked to the young men in reference to the organization of their Y. M. C. A., they became very enthusiastic about it, and shortly after my return home, came the information from Mr. F—— B—— that they had organized and were already engaged in active work; and no doubt through their earnest efforts, many of the young men who visit the public houses will be saved. I played and sang some pieces for them, after which the entire company joined in a farewell song which impressed me very much. In the company was the sister of my friend, Mr. R——, of Camden, N. J.; she was a woman of nearly four score years, but had retained considerable of her youthful spirit, and the young people enjoyed her society very much. That little company, which gathered in that quaint old house to bid the "Yankee" farewell, and give him their good wishes for a safe voyage across the Atlantic, will live in my memory, along with others of that little village whom I am free to call my friends. I asked Mr. F—— B—— how he would like to go to America; he said in a manner that amused the company: "I would like to go if I could go when asleep; I would not want to know anything about crossing the ocean."

MONDAY, August 13.—When I bade good-bye to Mr. G——, the invalid whom I have previously referred to, he said to me as he looked up into my face: "I shall soon be in that city where I will be entirely free from all my afflictions;" and as I looked at that man, so utterly helpless and yet so happy, felt I had been made the better for my having known such a character. I left the little village of South Littleton, feeling that my visit there had been one of pleasure, and also of great benefit to me.   Worcester was the next point of interest in view. This town is in the center of England and is beautifully situated, the river Severn dividing it. The Cathedral, which is a large and elegant structure, standing near the banks of the river, was built in 1034-1374. The dimensions given are 394 feet long, 72 feet wide and 162 feet high. The decorations are magnificent, and the fine stone pulpit in the choir is quite an ornament to the Cathedral. The monument of King John, is said to be one of the most ancient in England. I remained to a short service, which was sung by an excellent male choir. The large baptismal font made of wood, carved in the most artistic manner with heavy brass ornaments and spires reaching nearly to the arch above it, with carved figures of some of the saints on each side, I admired very much. I copied from a tablet the name of a lady who died in 1697, also that of Sir Thomas L——, and his wife,—the former died in 1650, the latter in 1666 ; also another of a man who died in 1674 ; Thomas S——, clerk of the city of Worcester, died in 1695. The chimes of the Cathedral are said to be very fine; the pieces used for each day are placed on a little bulletin board. I copied the ones that were there: "Home Sweet Home," "My Lodgings are on the Cold Ground," "God Bless the Prince of Wales," "Ye Banks and Braes." In the rear of the Cathedral are the ruins of an old abbey, overlooking the river. A gentleman gave me a short history of it. There is a subterranean passage leading from this abbey to a considerable distance under the city, but as I failed to jot down, in my note book, the account given to me of it, have lost the thread of some of the interesting facts connected with it. There is a beautiful little park besides the abbey, from which I had a grand view of the country on the opposite side of the river. The population of the city is about 40,000; several of the business streets present a good appearance. One part of the city is called "The Cross," deriving its name from the streets forming it. Visited the Y. M. C. A. hall, a neat little building on Copenhagen street, and the secretary seemed to be putting forth every effort to attract the young men of the city to this worthy place. From there went to the Royal Porcelain works; in going, passed through one of the most ancient looking streets that I had seen in all my travels. The little houses looked as though they were built many hundred years ago. At the entrance there is a show-room with a fine display of beautiful wares. The payment of a sixpence, entitled me to a guide book, and a visit through this interesting place. The celebrated Royal Porcelain ware is sold in nearly every market in the world. I was taken all through, from the mill to the finishing room, and was well repaid for my visit there. Left this ancient city at 4 P. M., and in a short time was in the familiar city of Birmingham, and was soon sitting at the old hearthstone at Harborn. Mr. E—— P—— took me to visit a wealthy bachelor, a particular friend of his. He and his nephew, a good, sociable young man, who with the exception of the housekeeper, were the sole occupants of this large and splendid mansion. When I was introduced to this member of the "bachelor's fraternity," situated as he was, confess I could not quite understand how it was he had held his membership in this worthy order so long.

Tuesday, August 14.—Took the 'bus to Five Ways, then walked down Islington Row, then to Great Colmore street, and called on the aunt of Miss P——, who had some messages and gifts to send to friends in America. At 1:20 p. m., left Birmingham on the Midland Railroad for Nottingham, where Mr. A—— M—— and Mrs. D—— lived, and who I had promised to visit before returning home. Nottingham has a population of 230,000, and is a very interesting city. I was directed to the home of Friend M——. He and I were soon on the tramp through the busy streets, and then went to the quaint old market-place, which covers about five acres, and I enjoyed the trip through it. We visited the famous old castle; it stands on a very high rock overlooking the city and river Trent, and from there I had a grand view of the valley of Trent. There is an excavation from the castle to the river; it is called "Mortimer's hole." There is a museum in the castle containing some relics which would interest any lover of old curiosities. At the entrance is a very nice park, where the children seemed to be having a good time. In the evening when we returned, found quite an excitement in the locality of my friend's home. The honeymoon of a bride and groom of a week, had suddenly terminated in a serious disturbance, resulting in her leaving without a very affectionate farewell. As the young bride passed us, returning to her father's house, I said: "She has found, like many others, that marriage is a failure." Some of the women took up the case and discussed it at great length.

WEDNESDAY, August 15.—Mr. M——, having shown me through some of the beautiful parts of the city, took me to Narrow Marsh, the White Chapel of Nottingham; there I saw some of the most depraved looking men and women that could be found anywhere. I cast my eyes about as we hurried through, and wondered how humanity could, in an enlightened land, sink so low. Nottingham is noted for its lace and hosiery mills, where hundreds of men and women are employed. One evening we came through one of the districts where a number of the mills are situated, just as the employes were coming from work, and the streets were so crowded that it was almost impossible for us to get through. Mr. B——, a brother-in-law of Mr. M——, is proprietor of a large lithographic establishment, which we visited and were much interested in, as Mr. B—— showed us the process of making their fine work. While there, was introduced to a Mr. L——, whose father is owner of a lace manufactory; he invited us to meet him at a given point, and he would take us through the mill, which he did, and we spent some time in watching them making lace, most of which was very handsome. We went to the park, which is quite a fine addition to the city; also visited the Cathedral cementry, under a portion of which are the caves where Robin Hood secreted himself when pursued by those who sought to bring him to terms. We spent some time looking at these old caverns, some of which look as though they were ready to collapse. On our way to the home of Mrs. D——, one of the ship's company, we passed through what was once the "Great Forest," and which bears that name yet, although the trees are very scarce. This forest is said to be where Robin Hood spent most of his time roaming around. The part of the city where Mrs. D—— lives is comparatively new, and the houses are very neat and pretty.

THURSDAY, August 16.—Went with Mr. M——'s mother to see some very old houses, which were built in the side of the rocks. The original rooms are cut in the solid rock, the fronts having been built at a more recent date. Mrs. M—— knew a family living in one of the houses, and the mother of the lady of the house, showed us through this quaint place. She was nearly eighty years old, and pointed out the room to us in which she was born, and also where her mother was born. She informed us that her mother lived there during her married life, her father having built the front of the house, and she had spent all her life there, her married daughter now having charge of it. In one of the rooms in the rock was a bedstead built close to the side of the rock, and this odd piece of furniture was two hundred years old. When I returned to Mr. M——'s, I found Dr. R—— there, whom I had not met since I left him in Edinburgh, Scotland, but had corresponded with him. His headquarters were at Long Eaton, a town a few miles from Nottingham. He came over to have me go home with him, but Mr. M—— had arranged a trip to St. Winford's Church, which stands near the banks of the Trent, about two miles from the city. In the afternoon Mr. M—— and I took this pleasant walk along the river to the church. Near by was a little town, the most of which were thatched roof cottages, giving it a very ancient appearance. As a matter of course I soon found my way into the old churchyard, and with book and pencil wandered among the tombs, copying the epitaphs that were out of the line of the ordinary. When we turned our steps homeward, the afternoon was nearly spent, and on reaching there found a Philadelphia *Ledger*, and perused it with pleasure.

FRIDAY, August 17.—After a visit to the home of Mrs. B——, sister of Mr. M——, I booked for Long Eaton, as I had promised to spend a little time with Dr. R—— before returning home. I was entertained at the home of Mr. D——, a friend of the doctor, where he had been stopping at intervals during his stay in England. This gentleman was a lace manufacturer, and in his home of wealth and refinement, I was made welcome at once. Dr. R——, Mr. D——, Jr., and I took a walk through the town. Most of the houses are large and handsome, with fine grounds. We called on some friends of theirs, and were entertained in good old English style. When I bade Dr. R—— good-bye, I discovered he was a trifle blue, and he said: "I am home-sick and wish I was going back to America with you," but in reply I said: "I am sick because I am not able to remain here longer, for there are yet many places I wish to visit." Booked for Trent, a short distance away, where after waiting for an hour for the train, started in the direction of Harborn. I was anxious to go to Northampton, where the gentleman lived who rendered me so much kindness on my first day in London, but was informed it would take me some distance out of my way, and my time was limited. When I arrived at the old home at Harborn, they were having an interesting game of lawn tennis in the field ajoining the house. Mrs. T——, a very estimable lady and an intimate friend of Mrs. P——, kindly presented me with a very handsome Bible and other valuable books before I left. She is a lady of considerable means and who, by her consecrated wealth, brings joy and gladness to many of Harborn's needy ones.

SATURDAY, August 18.—Mr. E—— P—— and I went to the free library at Birmingham; in one part is a museum in which was an idol from Hindostan, said to be two thousand years old. There were many other interesting old relics which we spent some time in looking at. The reading-room was the most complete of any I ever visited; there were papers on file from countries far and near, several of them being from different cities in America. Then went to a store similar to John Wanamaker's, but on a smaller scale. I purchased a hat, which my friends said was very becoming, but on reaching America, found there was a difference of opinion with my friends here in regard to the hat. One of my friends said, soon after greeting me: "Butler, you need more hat than that." After several comments of that kind, concluded to lay it aside as a souvenir of my trip. Mr. P—— joined us and we together took a walk through a part of the city that in all my tramping I had not visited before. In going through the old St. Phillip's churchyard, which is used as a thoroughfare, I found myself halting in front of some old time-worn tombstones and reading the epitaphs; in doing so, came across one of the most peculiar pieces of poetry I ever read, and which I copied. Mr. P—— said: "I have been coming through here for years and never saw that before." He was quite as much amused as myself. On returning to Harborn the entire family, with Mr. S—— F——, (who has since became a member of it), the tall Yankee, and Joe, the pet dog, were photographed in a group in front of the house.

SUNDAY, August 19.—Went to the Weslyan Chapel on South street, Harborn, and listened to a very earnest and practical sermon by a young local preacher. After hearing his excellent discourse, concluded he was on a fair way of becoming a full pledged minister. The service was similiar to that at City Road Chapel ; at the close I was introduced to several of the members by Mr. N—— whom I had met at his place of business in Birmingham. The superintendant of the Shenly Field Schools, at Northfield, and his wife, were intimate friends of the P—— family, and requested them to bring the American to visit them at this very worthy institution. So in the afternoon Mr. E—— P—— and myself took this very enjoyable walk, a distance of three miles to Northfield. We walked some part of the way along a splendid road passing some very quaint old farm house and then took a by-path across the meadows leading to the cottages which are situated on a hill, from which can be seen the tall church spires at Birmingham. The country in and around this place is beautiful, and on reaching the top of the hill, I feasted my eyes on the sublime scenery. The Shenly Field Schools, or home for friendless children, as we would style it, is conducted differently from any institution of the kind that I have any knowledge of. There are a number of cottages built of brick and quite attractive looking and nicely arranged for the purpose they were intended for. Each cottage is in charge of a man and his wife, with twenty children under their care; the children call them father and mother. The girls are thoroughly drilled in domestic affairs, and the boys are learned some mechanical business. They also have schools with an efficient corps of teachers, so that the children may, on leaving this institution, go out into the world prepared, in a measure, to meet its responsibilities. I understood that many children had gone from this place and grown up to be useful men and women, thus reflecting great credit on those whose care they were under. Mr. D——, the superintendant, and his excellent wife, seemed well adapted to fill this responsible position. As he showed us through the different cottages, I could see that he had the love and respect of the children, for as soon as they saw him coming their faces would light up with a smile, and the kind words dropped by him seemed to bring sunshine into their young lives; many of them were orphans, and others were children whose parents were dissipated and who possibly never knew what the comforts of life were until going there. He said to me: "I will take you to see my little ones after the matron has them snugly tucked away in bed." Some of the readers might think a visit there would not interest a bachelor very much, but it did. We were taken to the dormatory, where were long rows of neat looking beds, from which peeped the faces of little ones who had not the care of a loving mother, but a matron who seemed an excellent substitute for one. They ranged in age from about three years to five and six. There was a beautiful little flaxen haired girl about three years old, who attracted my attention; any father and mother would have been proud to have owned such an interesting child; Mr. D—— said she was bright and intelligent. There was a boy about the same age who had an unusually handsome face, and whose intelligence was remarkable. As I stood looking at those twenty little tots, they drew quite heavily on the sympathy of the bachelor's heart. They have a fine little chapel where they are taught which path to take leading to life eternal, and they also receive instructions along that line in the cottages. We sometimes say this is a cold world, but after knowing something of these institutions, both for young and old, that are found in great numbers on both sides of the Atlantic, and the Christian churches that dot our land and other countries, I am inclined to say that it has been warmed by our holy Christianity, until it is quite a comfortable place to live in. Mr. and Mrs. D—— are fine musicians and gave us some very good selections. We remained at tea and they insisted on us staying at supper, as the curate was to be there and they wanted us to meet him, but Mr. E—— P—— said: "Mr. Butler has only spent this one Sunday with us since he has been in England, and as I am to leave for Kent this coming week, to be away from home a long time, and we both want to go to the old Harborn Church this evening." So we started for home but found it was raining so hard we were compelled to return. Mr.

D—— informed us that their telephone was connected with the Christ Church in Birmingham, and we would be able to hear some of the service. At the time for service Mr. D—— called me to the telephone, and, as I placed my ear to it, heard the sweet strains of the organ, and, as I listened to the choir—which is considered one of the best in England—taking their part in the service, felt I was in communication with the heavenly country, particularly so when they sang one of the old, sweet, familiar hymns. I was so charmed that I reluctantly yielded my place at the telephone to others. When I again had the opportunity of listening the rector was just announcing the text; his voice had a musical sound, as it came over the wires to me with that gospel message. The sweet sounds of that service seems to linger in my ear yet. In a short time the curate put in his appearance; he was one of those kind of persons that a few minutes in his presence made you feel quite well acquainted with him. We sat down to an elegant repast at 9:30, and not only enjoyed what was set before us, but the pleasant conversation which was carried on at the table, none being more jovial than the curate. Soon after we wended our way through the midnight darkness, back to Harborn, reaching there about eleven o'clock. So closed my last Sabbath in England.

MONDAY, August 20.—Arose early and began preparing to take my departure from my English home, to which I had become much attached. Mrs. P——'s sister and brother-in-law, from Liverpool, visited Harborn during my trip to Antwerp and left a cordial invitation for me to spend a few days with them before sailing for home; and as there were but three days more to divide up between Chester, Oldham, Manchester and Liverpool, was obliged to be on the move early. With messages and a bundle of love to Fred. in America, I bade good-bye to my kind friends and hurried to Birmingham, and was soon speeding away, by the Great Western Railroad, to the old city of Chester; aside from the city of York, it is the most ancient-looking city which I visited. History informs us that there was a town on this site before the Roman invasion, but it was the Romans who made the definite foundations. The old walls, which were in ruins for about three centuries, were restored A. D. 907; a walk around them gave me some idea of the size of the city. While on the walls met four Americans—a lady and three gentlemen—who had landed in Liverpool that day, and enjoyed a pleasant conversation with them. They informed me they expected to remain in the country a year. I quite envied them. In going through some of the ancient streets was interested in looking at the curious carvings on some of the old houses; there are covered avenues above the streets, with a flight of wooden steps leading up to them, the stores being on the avenues above and below. I made a purchase at one of the stores—which is called, "The House of Good Providence," from the fact of it being the only house whose occupants escaped the terrible plague, a few centuries ago. It is said, the inmates of this house devoted themselves to caring for the stricken ones. The Cathedral, which is quite large, was begun in the twelfth century. Tradition says that a Roman temple to Apollo once stood on this site. I spent some time in wandering around through this old Cathedral. When I left Chester placed it on the list as one of the most interesting towns I visited. Arrived at Birkenhead at 6 P. M., crossed in the ferry boat to Liverpool, which place I had left three months previous. Took a Lodge Lane 'bus and rode through the busy streets to No.— Aspen Grove, where lived Mr. D——. I was received very kindly by him, his wife and her mother—who is also the mother of Mrs. P——, at Harborn. We spent the evening at the home of Mr. M——, brother of Mrs. P——.

TUESDAY, August 21.—Mr. D—— went with me to the office of the steamship company, to ascertain where the steamer sailed from. We then went to the Central Railroad Station, where I booked for Manchester, and from there to Oldham, a few miles distant, to make inquiry about relatives of Mrs. A——, a friend of mine in America. In conversing with a young man on the train, was informed that he knew one of the families I wished to see, and he directed me there. From this point was directed to her father's sister, and, like many of the others on whom I called with messages from America, she was so over-joyed that the great tears began coursing down her cheeks, as she said: "It is more than fifty years since my brother left home, and I have heard very little of him since." Made a hurried trip through the old town, which contains a number of manufactories. I saw a great many men and women coming from the mills; many of them wore clumsy looking shoes with wooden soles, which made quite a clatter as they brought them down on the pavements. On the top of a tram rode back to Manchester. It is built up all the way, from one town to the other, making one long street, so that you can scarcely tell when you reach Manchester. At the end of every mile, the conductor collected a penny. I asked him how many more times he would collect the fare, and, after informing me, said to him: "Let me drop the entire amount in the box, as I am going the whole length of the route," but he gave me to understand that he would continue to take it on the instalment plan. Manchester is a large manufacturing city, with a population of 500,000. Its streets were thronged with people hurrying to and fro, and as it was a fine afternoon, the ladies were out in full force, and had the right of way. Many of the stores are very large and attractive. I went, with a gentleman whom I met on the tram, through Lewis' immense store; it is one of the largest in the city and is run on the same principal as John Wanamaker's. From there I visited the Y. M. C. A., on Peter street. The assistant secretary showed me through their splendid hall; their lecture-room is very large and is lighted by electricity; the gymnasium is a very complete one. From there enjoyed a ride on the top of a tram, to the great ship canal; it was quite a long ride through one of the finest parts of the city. Some of the residences were magnificent, showing that the occupants had evidently succeeded in gathering a good supply of sovereigns. The canal is worth a visit, and I was quite interested in it, although having only a short time there. I expected to see a great number of ships at the quays, but there were only a few, from which cotton was being unloaded. The total length of the canal is 35½ miles; average width at water level, 172 feet, except between Barton and Manchester, where the width at water level is 230 feet; minimum width of canal at bottom, 120 feet; depth of canal throughout, 26 feet. From there returned to the business portion of the city and went through some parts of the new town hall, which is a large and beautiful structure. There are a number of very large, handsome buildings in the city. Left this busy place on the 6 P. M. train, arriving at Edge Hill, a suburb of Liverpool, at 7 P. M. On my way to the home of Friend D——, stopped at a shop, and, while the young man having charge was waiting on me, I engaged in conversation with him. He had a strong desire to go to America to seek his fortune, but said: "I can't go while mother is living, for I have to care for her." A very considerate son, I thought, and, whether he ever obtains a fortune or not, his mother has one in having such a boy. There was quite a company invited to the house of Mr. M—— to give me a farewell send-off, and I am sure I shall always remember, with pleasure, the last evening spent on the shores of Old England.

My Home Across the Sea.

(WITH MELODY ARRANGED.)

By Chas. J. Butler.

I left my dear old native land,
  To sail far o'er the sea;
And as our ship was seaward bound,
  Sweet home, I thought of thee.

Chorus.

My dear old home across the sea,
  How oft' my heart still turns towards thee,
Where e'er in foreign lands I roam,
  I'll not forget my dear old home.

Out o'er the ocean's dreary waste
  I gaze, and long to be
With cherished friends in home, sweet home,
  Across the dark blue sea.

Faces where kindness sits enthroned,
  I look upon each day,
But none that seem so fair to me
  As those far, far away.

In homes o'er Britain's isles, I've found
  A welcome at the door;
There's one awaits me in my home
  On old Columbia's shore.

Written at Sea, 1894.

Homeward Bound.

WEDNESDAY, August 22.—The day for sailing had come at last. We were on the move quite early, for the train left Lime Street Station, for the docks, at 9 A. M. Mr. D—— came with me to the station, and, having a little time before taking the train, spent it in looking at some of the places of interest in and around that locality. During my short stay in Liverpool, found it a much larger and finer city than I supposed when I walked through its streets the day I landed. On returning to the station, was pleased to meet Mr. T——, of Philadelphia, and Mr. F—— T——, wife and daughter, of Pittsburg, whom I met on the ship on the voyage across. We reached the docks at 10 A. M., and was soon busy packing my luggage away for the homeward voyage. In passing the companion-way, was utterly amazed to see Mr. Newton S——, of Camden, N. J., coming up the steps, not thinking of seeing any one from home. Seeing my surprised look, he said: "What is the matter?" "Well," I replied, "you are like one rising from the dead." He said: "I am too much alive to be coming from that region." We remained at the dock until about 2 P. M., then our noble ship slowly made her way, past the long rows of stone docks, into the river Mersey, and soon the last vestige of the shores of Old England disappeared. My room-mates were Mr. W——, a Philadelphia lawyer, and Professor P——, from the northern section of the city. Mr. P—— L——, of St. Louis, was to share our quarters with us on our arrival at Queenstown. We steamed into the Queenstown harbor through a dense fog, and when the mist rolled away had another good view of Ireland. The tender came out to our ship with quite a number of passengers; among them was the old man and his wife whom I have referred to as being so much affected when he caught sight of Old Ireland. They greeted us with as much pleasure as though we were old friends. When Mr. P—— L—— came into the state-room the first thing he did was to test the springs of his berth, and said to me: " I'm not pleased with it," and began to contrast the room with the one he had coming over. We were anxious to have Mr. N—— S—— room with us, as we were well acquainted with him and he was not pleased with his quarters, so I took the case in hand and had him meet Mr. L——; he invited him to his room in view of exchanging (I was there to help the thing along), and finally he concluded the berth would be preferable to the one assigned him. Soon I was doing the neighborly act of assisting Mr. L—— in moving, and in the meantime Mr. S—— was transferring his luggage to the "bachelors' sanctum"—for not one of the occupants of the room had, as yet, found a helpmate, and all, with the exception of Mr. N—— S——, had been in the world long enough to be styled bachelors. A number of small boats came out to our ship with persons having various articles for sale—blackthorn canes and shelalahs were their specialties. We were greatly amused at the manner in which they came on board with their wares; the men on reaching the deck would lower a rope with a large loop in it, in which the women seated themselves, and were hoisted on deck; it looked like a perilous undertaking, but they did not show any signs of timidity. Those that did not come on board would tie their wares fast to a rope and one of their number on deck would see that the customer passed over the cash and received the equivalent. They are pretty sharp in their dealings. A man in one of the boats was anxious to make a sale and held up a shelalah, fixing the price at four shillings. Some of the passengers "guyed" him by offering him considerably less. Just as we were about leaving Mr. T—— called to him and said: "I will give you three shillings for it." "You can have it," was his reply, in a good rich brogue, "if you'll come down and tussel with me for the other shilling." We left with Irish wit on the lead. We were soon on the bosom of old ocean, which a few hours later was being swept by a fearful storm, tossing our ship about, interfering considerably with the comfort of a large number of the passengers. I was the only one in our state-room who was indisposed and was on the shelf all one day. I made several attempts to show my seaworthiness, but betrayed myself each time by having to pay my compliments to "Neptune"—something that I did under protest. Tommy, the cabin boy, did his best to keep up my *stock*, in the way of toast and beef tea, but he finally gave it up, and *so did I*. Our ship's company was made up of very excellent people, and like those whom I had the pleasure of going over with, did what they could to make the homeward trip a delightful one. Among the number was a Mrs. B——, a lady more than "three score years and ten;" she was remarkably bright and intelligent and was the favorite of all who had the pleasure of knowing her; she was in company with her two daughters—one a teacher of elocution in Philadelphia, the other a Mrs. H——, a noted singer. Most of us were anxious to see land, but this old lady said to me: "I am so much in love with the old ocean that I am not anxious to have the voyage end," but as I had turned my face homeward, I was counting the days and wishing for the one that would bring us into the grand old Delaware river. I afforded a great deal of amusement to my three room mates, as I had a top birth and Mr. W——, who occupied the one beneath, was usually awake when I was ready to leave it, and made it rather difficult for me to reach the floor. Mr. N—— S—— was on hand to assist Mr. W—— in his good work, and I think, if the voyage had lasted a few days longer, I might have been well up in gymnastics. Mr. and Mrs. S——, a young bride and groom from Kent, England, were among our number. They were a very excellent couple and most of the passengers became quite interested in them and showed her a great deal of kindness when old ocean was behaving so badly and she was extremely ill. They were going to Kansas, to the home of their uncle, to begin life in the far west. I saw an opportunity of paying back some of the kindness shown to me while in the British Isles, and invited them to spend Sunday with me, as we expected to land on Saturday, and thought the rest over the Sabbath would fit them better for the long journey before them. They accepted my invitation and on Monday I was able to render them some assistance; as they were leaving Broad Street Station they said: "We will never forget our first Sabbath in America and the kindness shown us by the people we met in Camden, N. J. The Sunday in mid-ocean was one long to be remembered; it was one of the most perfect days I ever experienced; the sea was as calm as it was possible for it to be; the porpoises, in great schools, were sporting about the ship, some of them anxious to see what was going on in the outside world, judging from the way they bounded out of the water; we all watched them with a great deal of interest. The usual service was held in the saloon, most of the cabin passengers being present. Some of the familiar hymns found in Moody and Sankey's book were heard ringing out lustily from the steerage, and some one had the spirit of exhortation and was evidently being heard by his congregation, as his voice was well keyed up. Mr. M—— and son, and his cousin, Mr. C——, of Philadelphia, were returning from a trip to the Emerald Isle. Mr. M——, whom I became very well acquainted with (he sitting next to me at the table), informed me he had been on a visit to his home in the north of Ireland to see his mother; he said: "I shall never forget that parting scene; when I was about leaving she threw her dear old arms around my neck and wept bitterly, and I had to tear myself away and hurry down the road, not daring to look back." He is a successful business man in the northern part of the city. The days slipped by, and early Saturday morning, September 1, when I came on deck, found we were steaming up the Delaware bay. That word "home" never seemed so sweet to me before, and the old song, "Home Again from a Foreign Shore," which I had sung so often, never meant so much to me as it did that morning. It was more than sentiment to me; my feelings were entirely different from what they were three months previous, when the bow of the same steamer was turned seaward, bearing a lonely bachelor to a foreign land. Captain K——, an old friend of mine, who had charge of the government steamer, which brought the custom house officers to our ship, kindly invited Rev. J—— S—— and several of my friends, to accompany him on the steamer. The welcome which I received from the Captain and those friends, together with the one given me by the members and friends of the Bethany M. E. Church, Camden, New Jersey, is a picture that will hang on the wall of memory as long as the tall form of Butler is in the flesh. So endeth "A BACHELOR'S RAMBLES THROUGH THE BRITISH ISLES," in which I have endeavored to have my readers accompany me each day in my journey through the land beyond the broad Atlantic.

EPITAPHS

Copied from various Churchyards and Cathedrals in England and Scotland.

RALPH V——,
Died 1799, aged 24 years.
Thus death, grand monitor, oft' comes to prove,
'Tis dust we doat on, when 'tis man we love.

WM. J. M——,
Aged 10 years.
Silent be all my anxious fears,
My heart, no more repine;
Since Jesus, in His bosom, wears
The flower that once was mine.

RICHARD H——,
Died 1819, aged 42 years.
Ye thoughtless crowds that pass this way,
Think on your God while it is day;
For night will come and you will be
All in the dust as well as me.

WM. H——,
Died 1863, aged 63 years.
Old age and sickness brought me home
To the cold grave, where all must come.
Let old and young prepare to die,
In hope to live eternally.

ELIZABETH C——,
Died 1708, aged 62 years.
Pale death will hardly find
So good a wife so kind,
A mother in all her actions was kind,
They will not soon slip out of mind.

HARRY S——,
Aged 6 years.
A treasure lent not given.

JOHN V——,
Died 1797, aged 72 years.
Polite, ingenious, upright to the best of husbands.

WILLIAM R——.
Afflicted by our loss we lay you here
In silent sorrow, e'en your dust is dear.

SARAH W——,
Died 1805, aged 53 years.
Spectator consider; death
Will take you, judgment, will follow.

ALBERT D. J——.
While earth-born fades and dies
In darkness deep as midnight's gloom,
The white-winged scales the skies,
And lives in golden rapture there.

JOHN R——,
Aged 24 years.
A sudden change; at God's command he fell;
He had not time to bid his friends farewell.
Affliction came without a warning given,
And bid him haste to meet his God in heaven.

ROBERT T——,
Aged 34 years.
How short and vain are all our earthly joys;
One moment gives, the next perhaps destroys.
E'er I in wedlock closed the second year,
I saw the ghostly monster, death, appear,
Who, with pointed dart did pierce my breast,
And laid my feeble body here to rest
'Till that great day, when all shall rise again,
And place upon a level king with men.

SARAH C——,
In life respected, in death lamented.

HANNAH H——,
Died 1842.
She was—but words are wanting to say what—
Say what a woman ought to be; and she was that.

JAMES T——,
Died 1826, aged 19 years.
Observe my youth, note well the time
How death may take you in your prime;
Therefore on earth fix not your love,
Prepare to meet your God above.

JOHN R——,
Died 1847.
When at my life's last setting sun,
My conflicts o'er, my labor done;
Jesus, thy heavenly radiance shed
To cheer and bless my dying bed.

EDWARD C——,
Died 1787, aged 22 years.
Happy the youth who in his early years,
Obeyed God's word and shed repenting tears.
This fading world no pleasing charms can find
To stain his soul or captivate his mind.
Such was thy lot, blest youth, while here below,
But thou art gone far, purer joys to know.

JOHN H. M——,
Aged 50 years.
Who are so greatly blest,
  From whom has sorrow fled;
Who find such deep unbroken rest,
  While all things toil?—The dead.
The holy dead, why weep ye so
  Above their sable bier?
They are blest, they have done with woe,
  The living claim thy tears.

WANETTA S——,
Aged 39 years.

The smallest woman in the kingdom ;
Only thirty-three inches high.

ROSE K——,
Aged 21 years.

Passing stranger, call this not a place of dreary gloom ;
I love to linger near this spot, for 'tis my daughter's tomb.

SARAH R——,
Died 1822.

Here rests my wife now free from care,
Removed, I trust, from Satan's snare.
She lived in love, in peace she died,
I wished her life, but God denied.

JAMES B——,
Died 1781.

O, cruel death, how could you be so unkind
As to take him before, and leave me behind?
You should have taken both, if either,
Which would have been more pleasing to the survivor.

JOHN B——,
Died 1809, aged 34 years.

Stay, passenger, and look upon this stone ;
And stand, too, and ponder well where I am gone.
Death quickly took my life and sense away
And laid me down in this dark bed of clay.
Consider of it, and take home this line :
The grave that opens next may be thine.

J—— F——.

Our life is like a winter day,
Some only breakfast and away,
Others to dinner stay and are full fed ;
The oldest man but sups and goes to bed.
Large is his debt who lingers out of day ;
He who goes first has the least to pay.

Old England.

By Chas. J. Butler.

Old England stands forth firm and strong,
    With Ocean breaking at her feet;
Her arms outstretched to right each wrong,
    To all will justice kindly meet.

Where e'er sweeps Ocean's changing tide,
    Her white sails to the breeze are flung.
She walks with progress, side by side;
    Men list' and heed her silvery tongue.

In valleys, and on hill and plain,
    Are found the loyal, true and brave;
All o'er her wide and great domain,
    No shackels bind a human slave.

The dusky sons of India own
    The sway of England's noble Queen;
The Isles have long obedience shown,
    Though leagues of water roll between.

Long she has with unwearied hands
    Held up the Bible, God's great light;
Still for the truth she nobly stands,
    That book, the secret of her might.

Old England, ne'er thy trust betray,
    Long years ago God gave to thee;
Thy kingdom then shall ne'er decay,
    'Till Time's great wheel shall silent be.

Written in Old England, 1894.

CONTENTS.

	PAGE.
THE "SOUTHWARK," (Poem), ...	6
SEAWARD BOUND, ...	7
ON THE SHORES OF OLD ENGLAND,	26
MY FIRST NIGHT IN LONDON, ...	34
MY THREE WEEKS IN LONDON, ...	48
EN-ROUTE FOR SCOTLAND, . .	86
A TRIP THROUGH OLD IRELAND, ...	111
BACK AGAIN TO OLD ENGLAND, . . .	148
MY HOME ACROSS THE SEA, (Poem), ...	195
HOMEWARD BOUND, ...	196
EPITAPHS GATHERED IN ENGLAND AND SCOTLAND, .	202
OLD ENGLAND, (Poem), ...	206

www.ingramcontent.com/pod-product-compliance
Lightning Source LLC
Chambersburg PA
CBHW020901230426
43666CB00008B/1273